SPIRIT SPEAKS

Four Spiritual Stories

geoagape

Spirit Speaks:
Four Spiritual Stories
Copyright C 2016 geoagape
All rights reserved

Published by:
Spirit of Love's Way
7162 Kopp Road
Spring Grove, PA 17362
Email: spiritoflovesway@gmail.com

Printed in the United States of America

ISBN: 1539764907
ISBN 13: 9781539764908
Library of Congress Control Number: 2016918434
CreateSpace Independent Publishing Platform
North Charleston, South Carolina

DEDICATION

Since the ideas in these four spiritual stories were inspired by The Spirit of Love and were also written in the spirit of love, I dedicate this book to The Spirit of Love. I am grateful and humbled for the opportunity to be a communication companion and a vegan voice with The Spirit of Love.
May All Beings Know Peace and Love!
Namaste, geoagape

CONTENTS

Acknowledgements	vii
Introduction	ix
Elijah's Return	1
Gaia's Gift	37
Job's Daughter	49
Yeshua's Lamb	97
Never Again	111
Recommended Books	123
About the Author	124

ACKNOWLEDGEMENTS

I want to thank my parents Kathryn and David for their love for me through the years and their model of loving service with others.

I want to thank the "Rowdy Cowgirls" vegetarian community at Saint Paul School of Theology for nurturing my nine month process of becoming a vegetarian in 1981. I want to thank my brother Gary, my son-in-law Jay, and Dr. Will Tuttle through his great book <u>The World Peace Diet</u> for inspiring me to finally become a vegan in 2016. I want to thank the Vegan community of Myrtle Beach for their great food, nourishing companionship, and many wonderful laughs even as we struggle to raise consciousness, open hearts, and end the confinement, torture, slaughter, and consumption of our fellow earthlings.

I need to acknowledge the billions of non-human beings who needlessly suffer and die every year at the hands of human beings. Their suffering moves me to write and speak on their behalf and to be one of their many and growing number of vegan voices.

I want to thank one of my sisters, Katye Anna, whose three spiritual keys – "converge with others in love, you are responsible for your actions and thoughts which help create your reality, and we can only succeed together" – have been helpful in keeping me focused in co-creating my reality.

Finally, I want to thank The Spirit of Love for inspiring me to share these spiritual musings. I have done my best to give birth to these seeds of hope, light and love. I trust The Spirit will nurture these seeds of be-com-ing into manifest forms which will bless all.

INTRODUCTION

If you are familiar with Christian scripture, you've heard the phrase, "The wind blows where it will." The actual Greek word translated as "wind" is "pneuma" which also may mean "breath or spirit." Consequently, I like to say, "The Spirit blows where it will." We've all felt the wind on our bodies. I'm also quite sure we have all felt The Spirit moving in our midst even though we may not have recognized it as such. It might have been a walk through a mountain forest, sitting still with an ocean sunrise, listening to a sermon, basking in the glow of praise music, sharing thoughts and emotions with old friends, or even changing a baby's diaper.

I do believe the themes shared in the following musings were inspired by The Spirit. The phrase I use most often when I speak of The Spirit is "The Spirit of Love." I try to convey my love of the Earth and its sentient beings and my love for the Spirit in these musings.

The title for this collection of musings relates to the word "prophet" which may be simply defined as "speaking forth." While some see a prophet as "predicting the future" I primarily use it to refer to one who speaks forth the choices and consequences facing a particular people in a difficult context. While I cannot claim to be a prophet of biblical proportions, I can humbly claim that I, like many others called to be in ministry, do at times feel as if I am speaking what The Spirit of Love would have me speak in a particular moment. I humbly point to two personal incidents.

On that horrible day of September 11, 2001 my then wife reminded me of what I said eight years earlier after the first bombing of the World Trade Center. She said, "You were right!" I asked her, "Right about what?" She responded, "Don't you remember you said, 'They won't be satisfied until those towers are down to the ground.'" I can't say that I knew those words would come true. All I can say is she reminded me of breathing them. The idea of bringing the towers down to the ground was born in the first attack. Horribly, I had given voice to a possible future event which found resonance in the hearts and minds of heartless people. The spoken words became reality with the actions of people who created "A New Pearl Harbor."

I can also point to another event which I spoke about ahead of time and which I saw as possible if people chose it as their reality. Alongside the four short spiritual stories I'm including an editorial I wrote in 1984 at the invitation of my home-town newspaper while I was in federal custody for civil disobedience against nuclear weapons. In that editorial I spoke about a future meeting in space between Soviet cosmonauts and American astronauts wherein they would share bread and salt. At the time I wrote this editorial such a friendly sharing of bread in space seemed far-fetched. President Reagan was speaking of the Soviet Union as "The Evil Empire," scientists had a nuclear holocaust clock set just a few minutes before doomsday, and movies like "The Day After" instilled fear. But, I am happy to say, sharing bread and salt, which is a traditional Russian greeting, actually occurred several times in space by Soviets and Americans in the 1990's. I'm including the editorial because of its background information and its supportive relationship to these spiritual musings.

When I started writing these musings I asked a college friend who recently retired as an editor for a university press what makes a good story. She simply said, "Write well and have good ideas." I make no claims to being a writer of great literature. Honestly, I can only hope to rise to a respectable degree of mediocrity when compared to the greats. If I presented these stories in a college level creative writing class, I feel I would be lucky to receive a "gentleperson's C" for the writing component. Having said that, I make no apology for the ideas in these musings. In my humble opinion, the ideas are genuine, hopeful, creative, inspired, and loving. I trust that you will agree.

When I asked two family members to give a first reading to "Elijah's Return" my mother said it was "chilling" and my sister Sara said, "It gave me hope." Amazingly, I believe both responses are emotions I had hoped to encourage. The musing about Elijah being taken from and then returning to Earth twenty-eight hundred years later with a spaceship, not by a mistakenly described chariot of fire drawn by horses, was "given" to me around 2000 during one of the Introduction to the Bible classes I taught for my community college. I had already learned about "The Jerusalem Syndrome" while on my week long personal pilgrimage to Israel in 1995. I always kept saying, "I'll write it when I retire." When I retired in 2015 my excuse was no longer available so I commenced to be responsible for the inspired gift which was given to me by and in The Spirit of Love. I believe it's funny, engaging, creative, inspiring, chilling, threatening, and hopeful all at the same time. May Abraham's children be brought together to live in and share Peace with one another.

"Gaia's Gift" is the second short story. It is a simple, light, playful set of words giving expression to the hope for a cleaner, brighter, and more loving future for ourselves, our fellow "Earthlings," and the Earth itself. If you feel moved to share the poem by the same name therein during a future Earth Day celebration, The Spirit of Love will smile upon your gathering.

The third musing is entitled, "Job's Daughter." This is my humble attempt to wade into the great philosophical and theological theodicy debate about the justice of God. This story represents a great ongoing personal issue of mine in relationship with God and the created realm. Having written my Master's Thesis on Schopenhauer, the philosopher of pessimism, I've been wrestling with the idea of God as Creator for many years. As a minister I gave a three-part sermon series on the book of Job. In my college Bible classes I always enjoyed dramatizing Job's encounter with God as one of my seminary teachers did in our Old Testament class. I relished the time I could introduce Captain Dan of Forrest Gump fame, hanging onto the crow's nest in a violent storm challenging God to answer him. I'm grateful Joby received different answers in her short encounter than the defensive rationalizations given to Job. The responses given to Joby by The Holy One are answers with which I can live and hopefully you may find them more satisfactory too.

The last short musing is "Yeshua's Lamb." It's a simple, imaginary story of what the young Yeshua may have experienced if he got emotionally close to an unblemished lamb being raised for Passover. In this story I portray Yeshua as a Nazoraean Essene. I concur with the growing number of Bible scholars who contend that the biblical view of Jesus who is described as eating lamb and fish is not consistent with the historical Yeshua who as a Nazoraean Essene would have been against eating animals and against the sacrifice of animals and birds at the temple in Jerusalem. The book by Keith Akers, <u>The Lost Religion of Jesus</u> is a must read, in my opinion, if one wants to have a better understanding of the historical background of Jesus and his disciples. Whatever the truth may be concerning what Jesus did eat two thousand years ago, I can say with full confidence that if the "Shua" (I know him by that name) I know were alive and walking the Earth today he would be a vegan and would call for his disciples to be vegans like him. He would do so because of his compassion for the animals and our planet. My next writing project will hopefully be successful in convincing Yeshua's disciples, whether they are in the church or not, that following The Way of Yeshua includes the compassionate eating and consuming discipline of veganism.

The short, spiritual stories contained within were given by and received in The Spirit of Love. I share them with you in The Spirit of Love. May they be a blessing to you and yours. May they participate in bringing Peace to all beings and to our wonderful Mother Earth. May the Holy One bless you and keep you and yours. May The Holy One bless all the nations of the world.

May it be so.

Namaste, geoagape

ELIJAH'S RETURN

THE CHARIOT CALL

One – alone in the night,
stars over-head sharing their light,
then a voice from within, both far and near,
"ELIJAH, MY FRIEND, WHAT ARE YOU DOING HERE?"

"Lord, I don't know which way to go,
I wander wherever the wind it does blow.
Help me Lord, be with me now.
I'm seeking your will, please show me how."

"I HAVE A MESSAGE I NEED TO SHARE.
WILL YOU BE MY PROPHET, ARE YO READY TO DARE?
YOU NEED TO BE STRONG, YOU NEED TO BE TRUE.
ELIJAH, MY FRIEND, CAN I NOW COUNT ON YOU?"

"Lord, I am here at your will.
I am ready to fight, I am ready to kill.
Lord, give me your strength, I'll do your desire.
Send me your power, again send me fire."

"ELIJAH, WHY SPEAK OF FIGHTING AND KILLING MY FRIEND?
WHEN YOU KNOW MY TRUE HEART, YOU'LL KNOW THESE MUST END!
I HAVE SOME CHOICES THE WORLD NEEDS TO HEAR.
BUT THEY'RE NOT FOR THIS TIME, NOT FOR THIS YEAR."

"Lord, you speak in riddles, your words are not clear.
My family, my friends, I hold <u>them</u> dear.
There are those who hate me, there are those who hate you.
When they threaten us Lord, what else can we do?"

"ELIJAH, SOON YOU WILL SEE – THE CHOICES I'LL GIVE.
ONE LEADS TO DEATH, CHOOSE THE OTHER AND LIVE!
FOR THESE TO BE MADE KNOWN TO ONE AND TO ALL,
YOU'LL HAVE TO LEAVE THIS TERRESTRIAL BALL."

"Riddles again Lord, your words are not clear.
What is your purpose? Why am I here?
I'm not a bird with wings that can fly.
I'm bound to the Earth, I can't touch the sky."

"I WILL SEND YOU SOME HELPERS, THROUGH MY SPIRIT YOU'LL RACE.
YOU WILL LEARN MY TRUE WILL IN HEAVELY SPACE.
SO FAST YOU WILL GO THAT YOUR TIME WILL SLOW DOWN.
AFTER THOUSANDS OF YEARS, YOU'LL BE BACK ON THE GROUND."

"Whatever Lord, I don't understand,
But I will do what you want, guide by thy hand.
I am your servant, I hear and obey.
Show me your purpose, show me your way."

A few days later, Elijah and his attendant Elisha are walking in the Jordan Valley. One of several of Elijah's former band of prophets says to Elisha, "Do you know that God is going to take your master from you today?" "Yes I know, but I don't want to talk about it," Elisha responds.

As Elisha and the prophets watch, a whirlwind of clouds appears and Elijah is taken up in what appears to them as a chariot of fire drawn by horses of fire. But this "chariot" is actually a small transporter which quickly takes Elijah to a huge spaceship circling in Earth's orbit. Elijah is in for the ride of his soon to be extraordinarily long life!

A little grey being from outside of this solar system takes Elijah by the hand and shows him to a room where he is telepathically told to bathe and eat. The helper says to Elijah, "All will be explained to you soon. Now it is best to rest." Then he is shown a sleeping pod. Exhausted, excited, and confused Elijah soon falls asleep.

The "chariot of fire" bursts into light speed.

ELIJAH'S RETURN

Two thousand and eight hundred years later a whirlwind of clouds appears in the Judean desert and returns Elijah to the very spot from which he had been taken. Elijah watches as his helpers depart in the "chariot of fire" which had been undetected by Israeli and other armed forces because of its cloaking technology.

As the dust settles he hears the still, small, gentle whisper, "ELIJAH WHAT ARE YOU DOING HERE?" Elijah responds, "Your helpers have taken me up in your heavens. I have seen wonderful sights and I have grown in your wisdom of Love and Truth. I am not the same man who left this Earth twenty-five years ago. I left as a Jewish prophet seeing only from the viewpoint of my people and our limited understanding of you. Your covenant of Love embraces the whole universe. Our covenant of Love is now written upon my heart as Jeremiah prophesized. I seek only to know and to do your will. The voice says to Elijah, "GO TO THE TEMPLE MOUNT IN JERUSALEM. THERE I WILL GIVE YOU TWO VISIONS OF CHOICE WHICH YOU WILL SHARE WITH THE PEOPLE OF EARTH."

All too soon, this old Jewish man dressed in a wondrous white robe began attracting the attention of some Bedouins who had come out of their tents now that the whirlwind had passed. "Hey old man, what are you doing here?" a young man shouted. An older man came to his defense saying, "Where are your manners? Leave him alone, can't you see he's disoriented?" A third man quietly said, "We better get him out of here before the radicals know he's here."

A young man who had been visiting his family sees Elijah's situation and comes to his aid. "My name is Khadir. We need to get you out of here quickly. Sit behind me and hold on tight," he tells Elijah. After Elijah sits on the back of Khadir's motorcycle, Khadir races the engine and with dust spinning from the back wheel, Elijah's hair and robe are flying in the breeze. After a few miles Khadir stops at a secluded spot on the Jericho to Jerusalem road behind some big rocks in one of the road's famous curves.

Khadir says, "Who are you? What is your name? What are you doing out there in the desert all by yourself?" Slowly with his "heavenly" acquired English, Elijah states, "I am Elijah a prophet of God. God just told me I must go to the Temple Mount in Jerusalem and receive his visions of choice for the people of Earth." Khadir shakes his head and says, "Elijah the prophet. Well, you certainly look the part. So The Lord God told you to go to Jerusalem and receive some visions for the people of Earth!" Khadir mumbles to himself, shakes his head and says, "Okay, old man, I'll take you there. The authorities can deal with you. I believe you need a little R & R time in my wife's care. I have an important meeting to attend and I can't leave you here." Off they go up the winding road to Jerusalem – The City of Shalom, The City of Peace. Elijah smiles as his flowing long hair and lustrous robe dance in the wind.

As they enter Jerusalem, Elijah is amazed at how much bigger and busier Jerusalem had become. Buses, cars, trucks and army vehicles all catch his eye. Elijah's helpers had tried to prepare him for this new reality by having him view numerous images which had been received in space. They had also given him a quick history lesson of what had happened to Israel and the rest of the world in the time he had been gone. He even had learned some of his English by watching TV shows including "The Big Bang Theory." It was in that show in which he first heard the name Einstein. Elijah was told by his helpers that Einstein was correct in theorizing that time slowed down as speed increased for an object. Indeed, he was proof positive of it. 2,800 years later he was back on Earth only having aged about twenty-five years!

Khadir came to a stop by the Muslim Quarter Gate not far from the Temple Mount. "Are you sure you want me to drop you off here?" he asks Elijah. "The Lord bids it to be so," Elijah responds. Soon they are making their way through the winding, narrow streets until suddenly they turn a corner and they are facing The Wailing Wall. It stands before them as a marker of spiritual yearning and historical desolation. Elijah is struck by the dazzling sunlight reflected off of its white stones. He is inwardly moved by the radiant, holy energy he senses in this place. It's buzzing, it's alive with divine energy! Elijah knew from his "heavenly" teaching that the Temple he knew and loved had been destroyed by the Babylonians and a replacement had been built which was then destroyed by the Romans. He had already shed his tears in space for the Temples' destructions. Now, he raised his eyes and appreciated the exquisite beauty of the gleaming bronze dome and the blue exterior of the Dome which had been built in their place.

Gradually, the still, small, gentle whisper catches Elijah's heart. He hears, "ELIJAH WHAT ARE YOU DOING HERE? GO TO THE WELL OF SOULS UNDER THE ROCK OF THE DOME. THERE I WILL SHOW YOU THE VISIONS OF CHOICE YOU WILL SHARE WITH MY CHILDREN OF EARTH!" Khadir watches with suspicion as Elijah seemingly listens to the wind.

Suddenly, two Israeli Defense Forces soldiers approach them. One named David quickly asks, "Who are you? Show us your papers!" Khadir quickly complies and they thank him and quickly return his papers. Another asks Elijah, "Sir, where are your papers?" Elijah looks at him and says he has none. The soldier replies, "Who are you? Where do you live? Where is your family? What are you doing here?" Elijah quietly responds, "I am Elijah a prophet of God. I come from Tishbite in Gilead. Sadly, my family and friends are all now dead. God has told me I need to go to the Well of Souls and there I will receive God's visions of choice for his children on Earth."

The soldier replies, "Well you certainly look like I would imagine Elijah would look like! You dressed up well for the part! No papers. No ID. Simeon, I believe we have another Jerusalem Syndrome client here." Simeon replies, "You know I just started this detail here in Jerusalem. I remember it was part of the quick briefing I received, but I wasn't paying attention. I was focusing more on a cute, new, female soldier sitting in front of me." David replies, "You should have paid more attention! For decades tourists have been coming to Jerusalem to visit. Some who come are so overwhelmed by the emotions of being in The Holy Land that they temporarily lose their identity and believe they are a famous person from the Bible. We have them taken to a hospital which has a special unit built just for people with the syndrome. I've been told that for most of them it only takes one to two weeks for them to regain their identity. Unfortunately, there are some people who refuse the treatment and yet they create no problems living on their own or with friends they acquire. They've taken up residence in the city. A few years ago there was one lady who came into The Church of The Holy Sepulcher every day from nine in the morning until three in the afternoon and cried at the altar which holds the rock which some Christians believe is where Jesus was crucified. She really believed she was Mary the mother of Jesus. She never caused any trouble to anyone so the authorities let her alone. Nuts, huh! Well, the best thing for 'Elijah' is to get him off the streets, find out who he really is and reconnect him with his family and friends," said David. Khadir states, "David, I brought this man here because I too suspect him of suffering from the syndrome. Actually, my wife is one of the psychiatrists who works in that very unit. I knew the IDF would help me help 'Elijah' get the care he needs. You can hold him for at least two weeks on the restraining order to see if he poses a threat to himself or to others, correct?" "Yes Khadir, that's right," David responds.

Elijah is taken into custody by Simeon. David makes a call to his commanding officer saying, "Sir, we have another Jerusalem Syndrome patient here. We need an ambulance to pick him up for transport to the hospital." Khadir waits until the ambulance arrives and waves goodbye to Elijah. Elijah watches through the ambulance window as the Dome of The Rock disappears from his sight.

THE UNIT

Elijah is quickly transported to the hospital which specializes in Jerusalem Syndrome cases. Usually after seven to fourteen days of treatment the tourists are reoriented and are able to go back to their normal lives. Elijah is quietly escorted into the receiving room of the unit. A young psychiatrist says, "My name is Miriam. I understand you call yourself Elijah the prophet. We are here to help you. How did you get to the Temple area where you were detained?" Elijah responds, "A nice young man named Khadir picked me up in the Judean desert. He had a motorbike and gave me a wonderful ride." Miriam looks amazed and states, "You say a young man named Khadir! That happens to be my husband's name, he has a motorbike, and I know he was visiting his Bedouin relatives this morning. So my husband found you wandering in the desert and gave you a ride to the Temple Mount. Why did he take you there?" "Because The Lord told me to go there and wait for the visions he wants me to share with the people of Earth," responds Elijah. Miriam sat in wondering silence and then states, "Okay Elijah. I need to take you into the unit, orient you, and introduce you to some of your fellow residents."

geoagape

Miriam walks with Elijah into the treatment unit, shows him his room and then introduces him to other staff and a few of the other patients. Elijah first meets Peter, then Paul and then along comes Mary. He also meets people who believe they are Moses, Elisha, Jeremiah, Deborah the Judge, and even one who claims to be Jesus.

After Miriam leaves him in the Day Room, Elijah notices one patient sitting alone in the corner, He walks over and says, "I'm Elijah, who are you?" The patient responds in a whisper, "Vanity of vanities, all is vanity, all is just a chasing after the wind. We are but a mist – here today and gone tomorrow. You may call me Q, but some call me The Teacher. Elijah, how was your ride in the chariot of fire? How did the angels treat you? What was heaven like? Did you learn anything up there? They must have because you speak good English. So you are back after 2,800 years! Back for what? Did The LORD GOD tell you yet what you are to speak forth in the Holy Name? Ah yes, I can see in your eyes The Spirit has taken hold of you too and yet there is more to be known."

As suddenly as the sun appears on the horizon after waiting long for a sunrise, Q's demeanor changes and a different voice rises from the man's body. "You have to forgive my friend; he talks quite a bit and can be kind of a curmudgeon at times. My name is John, the beloved disciple of Jesus. The LORD has spoken with me about you and the mission you have been given. It is an honor to meet you Elijah. You are a good man, a great man! I can see it in your eyes. But you are also a troubled man with past blood on your hands. Scripture says you killed 850 priests after the Mt. Carmel confrontation. If true, that is a lot of blood on your hands – righteous or not! Elijah, surely God's heavenly messengers must have taught you the universe's primal teaching of Love?

God is Love; those who love know God, and Love forgives all." All of a sudden, John's facial expression changes and the voice of Q moans, "Vanity of vanities – all is a chasing after wind. Nothing has lasting meaning on this Earth. All comes to ruin. Even lovers lose each other in the dust of death." Then Q mournfully repeats in a sing-song voice, "Dusty wind, windy dust." Finally, he smiles at Elijah and states, "Catchy, huh! Someone should write a song about it."

Miriam comes to Elijah's side and quietly walks him away from the corner. She says, "Elijah, by now you have an idea of where you are and with whom you are. You are in The Jerusalem Syndrome Unit of a hospital. All of these people here, including you, believe you are a famous person from one of the Abrahamic religions. My job is to help you remember who you really are and to help you reconnect with your family and friends. You just met a patient in the corner who is unique in that he not only has the syndrome, but he also has a dis-associative personality complex. At one moment he believes he's the teacher from Ecclesiastes and the next moment he splits into believing he's the beloved disciple of Jesus. Usually, it takes just a few weeks for people to get well, but he's been in that corner for months now. My job is to let his real personality take control and help him say goodbye to his splits. You have to be hungry. The supper trays are coming through the door. Time to eat."

Elijah sits down at a table with Peter, Paul, and Mary who are always together. After saying individual prayers, Mary notices that Elijah has picked up the meat off his plate and wrapped it in a napkin. She says, "Midnight snack huh?" "No I don't eat meat," Elijah responds. "Why not?" Mary asks. Elijah replies, "In the last twenty-four years I've learned a lot about meat and its effect on our bodies, the bodies of host planets, and the uniqueness and value of every sentient life. I can see you are not agreeing with me. How about this. The Apostle Paul said the body is the temple of the Lord and we should treat it as such. I believe eating the flesh of animals harms the spiritual temple of a human being's body." Paul suddenly exclaims, "Yes, I did write that, but I also disagreed with James and the other Nazoraeans that one must be a vegetarian if one wants to live a spiritual life. Holiness is not determined by what goes into the mouth, but by what one believes in their heart." Elijah quietly responds, "The friends I lived with for the last few years showed me how to live in love with all that is. I finally came to feel the suffering of animals which were raised and slaughtered only to feast our taste buds. They even taught me that the old temple sacrifices were not ordered by God. They showed me the words of the prophets who came after me like Isaiah, Jeremiah, and Amos who rejected the blood sacrifices, but instead called for a pure heart of compassion for all being." Mary exclaims, "I couldn't live without meat. I eat meat three times a day. The Dalai Lama eats meat!" Elijah continued by saying, "Meat is bad for the Earth and I've seen whole planets destroyed by the meat eating and the consumer choices of their inhabitants which changed the climates of their planets irrevocably. Earth is reaching that tipping point. Animals produce methane gas. They take up huge amounts of fresh water. The ocean's fisheries are declining. The rain forest is disappearing so crops can be planted to feed cattle. My guides showed me the Earth is getting more and more fragile as an ecosystem and we need to love her and live as gently as possible on her." Silence overwhelmed the table partners giving everyone something to chew on.

Elijah leaves the table and returns his tray to the dinner cart. He sees the TV reporting the day's news in Israel, Palestine, and around the world. He solemnly shakes his head and returns to his room. Elijah prepares for sleep. Suddenly, the gentle whisper wraps around him, "ELIJAH, WHAT ARE YOU DOING HERE? GO TO THE TEMPLE MOUNT! GO TO THE WELL OF SOULS! Elijah looks out of his room's unbreakable window and sees the nearly full moon which reminds him that a rare "blood moon" – a lunar eclipse – will occur in two days. He marvels at the timing for that will also be the day of Passover.

THE PRAYER

That night Miriam and Khadir have a conversation about meeting the man who called himself "Elijah the Prophet." Miriam said as she reclined in bed eating vanilla ice cream with chocolate covered pretzels, "It's amazing that you were the one to rescue him from the desert. He could have died out there from the animals or the radicals." "You knew I needed to see my family after such a long time not being with them," he responded. "My teaching is going well and now was a good time to visit. He's really a confused guy. He really believes he's the real prophet." Miriam says, "He's different from most of my patients in the unit. Within a few hours you can see most of them wavering in their identity claims and you can see some indecision in their responses. I saw none of that with this Elijah. He met a lot of the other patients and he laughed at the thought of meeting Moses, Peter, Paul, and Mary. He really enjoyed meeting Thomas/Q/John, the craziest of them all. Oh! The baby just kicked. Feel it! It's really active tonight. Say 'Hi' to daddy. Khadir tenderly touched Miriam's belly and laughs as the little one bounces off the walls of her maternal cave.

geoagape

As an interfaith couple their life together is an example of how love can bind together people of different faiths. An Israeli, Jewish, psychiatrist and a Palestinian, Muslim, physics teacher laugh as their little one pushes the maternal envelope. Miriam smiles and says, "So what are we going to name our baby?" Khadir gives her a kiss on her forehead and says, "It's too soon. Let's just let The Spirit of Love help us know the right name when the time is right. We don't even know the sex of the child yet." Miriam replies, "No, we'll be so busy when he or she arrives. We should name our love child now." "Maybe we should just name it 'love child,'" Khadir suggests and laughs. "Honey, a word in Hebrew for love is 'ahava.' What's a word in Arabic for love?" Miriam asks. "Well, one word that's used is 'habibi.' Hmmm, 'habibi' and 'ahava.' Maybe we could name our love child 'Habihava' or 'Havabibi,'" Khadir suggests as they both giggle. They look at each other quietly for a few moments, smile with each other, and say at the same time, "Aha! Ahabi!" Miriam laughs and states, "I really like it; it blends our traditions. We give our lovechild a new loving name! Ahabi! Boy or girl!" Khadir kisses Miriam on the lips and then raises her shirt and kisses her belly saying, "Hello little lovechild! Daddy and mommy just created a loving name just for you – Ahabi. Sleep well little one, Daddy and mommy love you."

After some joyful silence Miriam asks, "Khadir, you are a physics teacher. In my philosophy class many years ago we once read that Einstein postulated that as things speed up time slows down for them. So isn't it theoretically possible for someone to go into the future? Say a spaceship picked up the real prophet 2,800 years ago and did that movie time/space jump into warp speed thing, isn't it possibile that the guy in the unit could be the real Elijah? The Tanak says he was carried into the heavens by a chariot of fire; maybe that was their way of describing a spaceship! Khadir laughs and says, "Theoretically speaking it's possible and there are some equations to suggest if they stayed at or near the speed of light for about, hmmm, let's say about twenty-five years of his time they could slow down and return him to our time, 2,800 years into his future. So yes, it's possible, but it's highly improbable that Elijah is here in our midst. Boy, wouldn't that make a great movie!" Miriam smiles and kisses him gently on the cheek and says, "The scriptures say that Elijah will return before the Messiah comes. They also say the Messiah will bring a reign of peace. Wouldn't that be wonderful – a better world for our little Ahabi."

Khadir nods and says, "You and John have such nice imaginations. It's getting late. Let's say our prayer." They faced each other and placed their right hands over each other's hearts. Then they covered their lover's right hand with their left hand. Together they prayed the Spirit of Love prayer they learned while at a spiritual retreat for couples:

"As above, so below, Light and Love sow and grow.
 One through space, one through time, one in Spirit, Love sublime.
  Holy Spirit, Heavenly Dove, Breathing Light, Breathing Love.
   Everyone, Everything, Earth's Love, Empowering."

With each line they imagined the symbols they were taught by the retreat leader which empowered the letters in the word "LOVE." For the letter "L" they imagined Jacob's ladder stretching from Earth to Heaven with angels descending and ascending. For "O" they saw within themselves at their third eyes pulsating, concentric circles. For "V" they imagined a Dove of Love hovering above them. Finally, for the letter "E" they imagined they saw a line proceeding from an imaginary center going up towards twelve o'clock and ending in a heart shaped "e" before returning to the center and then they saw three more imaginary loops at the six, three and nine hour positions. The final image looked like two infinity loops with hearts at the end of each. For several minutes they sat in the wondrous Power of Love. Then they opened their eyes and fed each other's soul. They hugged each other, darkened the room, and fell asleep in each other's arms.

The little one within Miriam always loved when her parents prayed this prayer of love. She couldn't wait until she could feed her parent's souls and be fed by theirs in this intimate sharing of spiritual love. She too joined her parents in sleep with the Dove of Love covering them all. If an ultrasound would have been taken as Ahabi fell asleep the technician, but not the parents, would have been joyously surprised to see her little right hand pressed close to her heart with the left hand on top.

THE GROUP SESSION

Upon rising, Elijah said his prayers, ate breakfast and then joined in his first group therapy session. Miriam welcomed everyone and then said, "First, I want to introduce you all to a new member of the group. He calls himself Elijah." Quickly, the one who calls himself Elisha shouted, "O Master, it is good to see you again. Thanks for giving me a double portion of your Spirit!" Elijah calmly looked at him and said, "I served with Elisha. I knew Elisha. Elisha was a friend of mine. Sir, you are no Elisha." The one calling himself Elisha was struck by what was said and in a flash of recognition came to his senses remembering his true identity. "Elisha" thanked Elijah for the reality check, rose from the circle and left the room with an attendant.

Peter said, "Welcome Elijah. It's about time you've come back. Malachi prophesized that you would be sent back before the great and dreadful day of the Lord, so the Messiah's return could now be at any moment. The scriptures say now is the time for you to 'turn the hearts of fathers and children to each other.'"

"Peter, I am here to receive some visions from The LORD and to share them with the people of Earth," Elijah stated. Paul exclaimed, "Good, good! I know a man who had visions! He went to the third heaven and saw things that can't be spoken of." Mary laughed and said, "Paul we all know you're talking about yourself when you say that!" "Vanity of vanities, all is vanity! Visions come and visions go. Visions are as a mist in the air. Even if the LORD spoke from the heavens few would believe. They'd say, 'it is Hollywood special effects.' There is nothing new under the sun. Death, disease, destruction, demons, war, famine, earthquakes, greed, poverty, sexism, racism, classism, abuse, and the beat goes on. Too little love, too late," moaned Q.

Miriam sighed and said, "Q, we all know your beliefs. Can you let John speak?" "Of course I can speak" responded John. "I know I'm supposed to love everyone, but can you imagine what it's like living with him in the same body all of these months? He means well, but all he needs is a good friend or companion to give him a little tender loving care. He forgets about saying the best we can hope for is to sit under a fig tree with the person you love sharing a loaf of bread and a jug of wine. Ah, that simple mention of bread reminds me of Shua, my beloved. A meal of Love. Agape. Little children, love one another. It's all about Love. The Beatles got it right, you know."

Suddenly, an alarm bell sounded and everyone was escorted into an inner room which served as the unit's bomb shelter. The radicals' rocket range had recently advanced so much that now it had the City of Peace within its reach. This time the rockets fell short, but several miles to the south precious blood was again spilled on the ground.

ELIJAH DREAMS

That night Elijah had many dreams of his younger life. He hears himself cry out to the LORD, "Take my life from me now, I have had enough. I am no better than my ancestors." He dreams of the miracle of the endless pot of meal and bringing back to life the widow's son. He dreams of the forty days in the wilderness after being fed by ravens. He dreams of that awesome night on Mt. Horeb where a great earthquake, a great wind, and a great fire made him fear for his life, but the LORD was not in them, but was instead in the still, small voice, the gentle whisper, "ELIJAH, WHAT ARE YOU DOING HERE?" He has nightmares of the Mt. Carmel murders and the blood soaked ground. He dreams of the Chariot of Fire and being lifted into the heavens. He dreams of learning the universe's wisdom teaching shared by civilizations long dead. He dreams of meeting Jesus alongside of Moses on a mount in Galilee. He dreams of being given by his parents to the holy band of prophets and being raised by them. He remembers the gentle whispers and the other voice that wasn't as gentle nor as quiet. He dreams of seeing the Earth from his "chariot" as he left Earth and again as he returned.

At three in the night he awakes to the gentle whisper, "ELIJAH, WHAT ARE YOU DOING HERE? GO TO THE WELL OF SOULS!" "LORD, I am in a locked ward. I need a little help here. Provide me a way out and I am ready to obey." Elijah hears no more sound. Slowly, sleep returns, and this time he sleeps in the peace of one who knows whose he is.

THE THREE IN ONE

Elijah awakes from a deep and restful sleep and joins Q/John in his corner. He hears Q say, "To everything there is a time and purpose under heaven. A time to be born, a time to die, a time to laugh, a time to cry, a time to mourn, a time to dance, a time for war, a time for peace." Following a long silence Elijah hears Q continue, "Wisdom is better than weapons of war, but one sinner destroys much good." Elijah nods his head and pats Q on the shoulder.

A few minutes later John speaks, "I remember when he said, 'A new commandment I give you, love one another as I have loved you. As I have loved you, love ye one another. By this know that you are my disciples, by the love you have for one another.' God is Love. Yeah. God is Love." Elijah again nods his head and pats John on the shoulder.

Elijah quietly says, "Q/John you are two old souls incarnating in this body with which another soul was born, isn't that correct? Can I speak with the soul who had this body before you two invited yourselves to join the party?" Q/John respond, "We'll check and see if he wants to talk." A time of silence follows, but then a new voice speaks, "Hi Elijah. Thanks for asking to speak with me. I been so overwhelmed by what has happened to me with their entrances. I just got so frustrated that I kind of shut down." "What's your name?" Elijah asks. "My name is Thomas, which is somehow appropriate because it means 'twin.' But in our case maybe we should be called 'trinity' because we are three in one. Bad joke I know, but you have to laugh at something, right!" "What's it like playing host to Q and John?" Elijah asks. Thomas replies, "Well it's really crazy. I hear everything they say. John's not bad, but Q keeps going on and on. It's like having Schopenhauer and Mother Teresa as best friends, but never being able to say 'go home.'"

Elijah calmly pats Thomas on the shoulder and says, "I believe they are here in you, speaking from you, because they and you are here to help me somehow. I'm not sure yet what it will be, but my spirit says The LORD is going to use us all together in the future, somehow." "How could I help you?" Thomas asks. Elijah replies, "The LORD will show us the way."

THE DEMONSTRATIONS OF POWER

A few hours later, Elijah met Miriam in her office for an hour of reality therapy. Miriam said, "It's good to see you again. How was your night?" Elijah shared, "I dreamt of my past. I've helped a lot of people, but I also have a lot of blood on my hands. Miriam, I am Elijah the prophet. I wasn't taken up in a chariot of fire as the Bible states and the song words sing. It was a spaceship. We went into light speed and instead of dying 2,800 years ago I aged only 25 years and my light helpers set me back down. Einstein was right! God wants me to go to the Temple Mount and receive two visions – choices that detail the consequences of the two paths that lie ahead for the people of Earth."

"Elijah, I know that Einstein has this theory, because my husband Khadir, the man who picked you up in the desert, is a physics teacher and we talked about the possibility of you being the real Elijah. He says it's possible, but highly improbable. I must say though, I've helped hundreds of people with Jerusalem Syndrome, but you are somehow different. There's just something about you. Oh! The baby is really jumping. It was quiet until we started talking. Maybe it likes the sound of your voice! I just wish there was some way I could know for sure; I feel that I'm a little crazy myself just talking like this" said Miriam.

Elijah became very quiet and then calmly said with his eyes closed, "Last night you and Khadir were talking in bed about me. You had vanilla ice cream and instead of eating it with a spoon you used pretzels that were coated with chocolate. It was a nice pregnancy snack for you! He had on a favorite shirt of his that says, 'Schroedinger's cat walked into a bar or did he?'" Elijah laughed and said, "I have to admit that's funny! You had on a favorite shirt that states, 'My inner curmudgeon and I are still debating.' That's funny too, but not as funny as his. You talked about the baby's name, but he said to wait and the Spirit of Love would give it to you when the time was right. But then you decided to name your love child with a name you created. Ah, Ahabi! I like it. Nice way to demonstrate your love for each other and your different traditions! You then placed your right hands over each other's heart and prayed a wonderful and powerful prayer which invokes the Spirit of Love." Elijah opened his eyes and moved his hand closer to Miriam's child. "You have been blessed with a girl. Ahabi will grow up to be a powerful servant of Love, if she chooses the right paths." Miriam looked at Elijah with awe and amazed wonder as her eyes filled with tears.

Suddenly, the bomb alert system sounded and everyone began running for the shelter, but before they are out of the office a rocket explodes into the unit scattering debris and bodies across the unit. As they enter the hallway, Elijah sees the Director of the unit lying on the ground with a massive amount of blood on his chest. Miriam checks his pulse and says, "He's gone. There's no pulse, and he's not breathing. Come on, we need to save ourselves." Elijah steps over the Director and says, "O LORD, my God, I pray thee, let this man's soul come back into him again." With a sudden gasp of air the Director opens his eyes. Miriam looks at Elijah with awe and trembling and asserts, "Now I know you are a prophet of God and that the Word of the Lord in your mouth is true." The Director looks at Elijah and Miriam and weakly states, "I was in the Light, but Elijah's prayer brought me back. I was told to tell you to leave now and to take Elijah and Thomas to the Temple Mount." They helped the Director to the unit's shelter where nurses took him in. They found Thomas quietly sitting in the corner with Q muttering, "A time for war, a time for war, a time for war." Miriam shouted at him, "Thomas, get up! You are going with Elijah and me now! We're leaving the unit! Get up and follow us!" Thomas got up and as they walked down the hallway choked with smoke and debris, Miriam and Elijah heard John say, "A time for love? A time for love? A time for Love?"

THE TEMPLE MOUNT

Driving through the streets of Jerusalem, taking detours where necessary, Miriam calls Khadir on her cell phone. "Honey, I'm okay, but the hospital has been hit by a rocket and I left. There's death and chaos, but the Director told me to leave and bring Elijah to the Temple Mount. Khadir, I know how crazy this sounds, but it's really him! Einstein was right! A spaceship picked him up and brought him back! Elijah is here! He told me what we did last night, what we ate, what we wore, what we prayed. He told me we chose the name Ahabi for our baby girl! The Director was lying dead in the hallway, but Elijah's prayer raised him back to life again! You have to believe me, Elijah the prophet is here! Call your friend Habib who works at the Temple Mount. Tell him 'Elijah is here!' Tell him what I just told you. He's a Sufi and we both know what a devout spiritual man he is who wants peace as much as we do. Khadir, he has to believe us! Elijah is here! Elijah says God needs him to go to the Well of Souls where he will be given two visions, two choices, for the people of Earth. I'll meet you at the Muslim gate. It's really true! Elijah is here!"

Fifteen minutes later, Miriam arrives at the gate and sees Khadir and Habib waiting. After exiting the car, Habib and Elijah calmly look into each other's eyes and souls. Finally, Habib puts his right hand over his heart, then placing them together he bows towards Elijah and says, "Welcome back home Elijah! May I escort you to the Well of Souls?" As explosions continue booming, sirens continue blaring, and jets continue blasting overhead in the sky, Habib leads them through gates which he unlocks and quickly they make their ascent to the top of the Temple Mount and into the Dome of the Rock. With great haste they descend into the Well of Souls underneath the rock. Miriam, Khadir, and Thomas wait at the entrance while Habib escorts Elijah into the center of the cave and then backs ten steps away with his head bowed. Miriam, Khadir, and Thomas watch with awe while breathing heavily.

Elijah kneels, bows forward with his brow to the ground and prays. Soon the ground trembles and a golden shimmering light begins to fill the room. Elijah hears the still small voice:

"SEE NOW MY SERVANT, THE VISIONS OF CHOICE,
IN ONE WE WILL MOURN, IN THE OTHER REJOICE!
ELIJAH, MY PROPHET, TWO CHOICES I GIVE,
ONE LEADS TO DEATH, IN THE OTHER THEY'LL LIVE!"

THE VISIONS OF CHOICE

While still kneeling Elijah raises head and sits in a posture of meditative prayer. His hands are folded in his lap with his palms facing upward. Suddenly, two figures, a woman and a man, clothed in radiant white, appear behind Khadir, Miriam, and Thomas. They smile, bow to them, and calmly walk by. Habib feels their presence, exchanges smiles and bows with them, and steps back to stand with Miriam, Khadir, Thomas, and Ahabi. The two stand by Elijah, one on either side, with their glowing faces directed towards the entrance in a posture of protective peace.

Slowly, the atmosphere within the Well of Souls changes and the four doorkeepers feel the need to kneel and bow their heads to the ground. They are experiencing the powerful presence of The Holy One. Knowing that the beings in white are guarding the Well, they close their eyes and begin to pray. Within five seconds their eyes begin to rapidly move up and down indicating they are in Theta wave-land. Miriam, Khadir and Thomas begin to experience small portions of what Elijah is experiencing, but Habib, Q, John, and Ahabi are experiencing much more, yet not all.

Elijah's soul is lifted from his body and taken to the Mount of Ascension which overlooks the Temple Mount and Jerusalem. He hears within, "SEE THE FIRST VISION!" Elijah sees and hears explosions all around him. Black clouds of death are boiling through the sky. Quickly, Elijah is soaring over the city. Muslims in their quarter, Christians in their quarter, and Jews in their quarter are dead and dying in their homes and in the streets. Men are screaming, children are sobbing, and mothers are wailing for children torn apart. Blood again is running as rivers in the City of Peace – The City of Shalom – The City of Salaam. A great explosion attracts his attention. Elijah is horrified by what he sees. The Dome of The Rock has been demolished by one well-placed bomb from above. The explosive force of the bomb is also enough to cause The Wailing Wall to crumble to the ground. Two spiritual centers which stood for centuries are gone in one second. Rising higher above the city Elijah is buffeted as jets blast by.

The experience is too much for Miriam, Khadir, and Thomas. Wailing tears of sorrow, their souls beg to be released from experiencing the small portions of the vision of death which they were enabled to share. In compassionate kindness, the female guardian lifts her hand and projects a beam of light which cuts their connection with Elijah's vision. They crawl just outside and to one side of the cave's entrance, bow their heads, and hug each other tight. Habib continues to kneel and receives small portions of what Elijah is experiencing.

Slowly, Elijah rises from merely hovering over the city and soon he can see tanks firing on each other in the Golan Heights and on the Egyptian border. He rises further and soon he can see the curvature of this beautiful blue planet. He remembers this beautiful sight from his ride into space. He is shocked by what now appears before him. A nuclear explosion appears over the border of Israel/Palestine and Syria. He does not know who is responsible for the explosion. Within minutes, Elijah sees nuclear explosions over

geoagape

Iran, Saudi Arabia, and more explosions over Israel/Palestine. Elijah is horrified to see cities with millions of people being evaporated within seconds. Tehran, Mecca, and Jerusalem are gone. The Ka'ba, The Dome, and The Wailing Wall have been vaporized.

Rising higher still, Elijah begins to see scores of nuclear mushrooms rising from more areas of the Earth. He sees explosions in Turkey, North and South Korea, Japan and China, Pakistan and India, and Eastern Europe. Finally, Elijah sees a multitude of mushrooms over Russia and the United States. Moscow, Washington D.C., New York, Paris. London, Berlin, Chicago, Los Angeles, and the missile fields of America and Russia are boiling in nuclear hells. All of these great cities and all of the vaporized people therein are added to the names – Hiroshima and Nagasaki. Elijah weeps without ceasing.

Gradually, the dark madness of the first vision, the first choice, the choice of death fades from his inner sight and Elijah's soul settles back into his body. Soon a cleansing breeze blows away the heaviness of the dark, dense, dance of death he has just witnessed. He again hears the still, small voice within: "ELIJAH, NOW WITNESS THE SECOND CHOICE, THE CHOICE OF LIFE." In a series of scenes, Elijah is taken to many joyous celebrations of love and peace. In the first he sees a young girl speak to the United Nations and the people of Earth about The Way of Love based on the prophecy of Isaiah in which he saw nations laying down their weapons of war and turning them into tools of peace. He sees leaders of the nations bringing symbols of war and melting them in a fire by Isaiah's statue which stands in front of the United Nations building. In another vision Elijah sees the Lion of Israel/Palestine lie down with the Lamb of Jerusalem as both governments, through real peace talks, decide to make the old city of Jerusalem an international city under the supervision of the UN and both decide to build their capitols just outside of old Jerusalem in order "to give peace a chance." In another vision he sees people in different parts of the world sharing the bounty of the Earth's plant life from community gardens, giving as they are able and taking what they need. They break bread with each other in animal free meals of joy and thanksgiving. He sees people of different hues blending in a rainbow dance and song. Elijah weeps tears of joy. Habib's tears join Elijah's on the floor of the Well of Souls. Slowly, Elijah hears the still, small voice whisper within his heart:

"THE TIME HAS NOW COME, ELIJAH MY FRIEND,
THE EARTH DRENCHED IN BLOOD THIS MADNESS MUST END!
TAKE MY VISIONS OF CHOICE, TO ALL FAR AND NEAR.
LET'S HOPE EYES WILL SEE, LET'S HOPE EARS WILL HEAR.

STOP FEEDING THE DEMONS OF BLOOD AND YOU'LL SEE,
THAT WITH LOVE ALL AROUND, REPENTFUL THEY'LL BE.
MY CHILDREN OF PEACE WILL ALL LEAD THE WAY,
TO AN EARTH FILLED WITH LOVE, WHAT A GLORIOUS DAY!

MY PROPHETS AFTER YOU HEARD LOUD AND CLEAR,
WHAT IS MY WILL, WHAT I TRULY HOLD DEAR.
I WANT MERCY AND COMPASSION FOR ALL,
WHO BREATHE IN MY SPIRIT ON THIS TERRESTRIAL BALL.

I WANT NO BLOOD SACRIFICE – THE KILLING MUST END!

LITTLE ONES ARE GROANING, THEIR HEARTS WE MUST MEND.
THE FALSE ONES WANT BLOOD THROUGH MEAT AND THROUGH WAR,
EARTH DRENCHED IN BLOOD, BOTH NEAR AND SO FAR.

ISAIAH WAS RIGHT, MY DREAM IS STILL TRUE.
A CHILD WILL SHOW YOU – HOW TO LOVE – WHAT TO DO.
THE TIME HAS NOW COME FOR ALL WHO WILL CARE,
TO HELP MY EARTH BE ONE HOUSE OF PRAYER.

WHATEVER YOUR FAITH, WHATEVER YOUR CREED,
LOVE IS THE ANSWER TO EVERYONE'S NEED.
I THIRST TO SEE FROM MY HEAVEN ABOVE,
THE EARTH BECOME A TRUE GARDEN OF LOVE.

Elijah sat in the peace which passes all understanding. The figures in white bowed to Elijah and then left the Well. Habib, Khadir, Miriam, and Thomas surrounded Elijah in a primal group hug as a gentle wind miraculously surrounded them. Suddenly, they hear explosions above them prompting Habib to say, "We must leave and get to safety. The Spirit is guiding me to take us all to my spiritual community. I trust that with the Spirit's guidance and the will of Allah, we will find safety there." They all followed Habib up the stairs, into the Dome and out into the smoke-filled light of dusk. Elijah was relieved to see that his vision of the Dome's and Wailing Wall's destruction was still only a possibility for the future.

COMPANIONS IN THE SPIRIT OF LOVE

After a dangerous three hour drive north, Habib reached the entrance of his spiritual community which was set in between the eastern base of Mt. Carmel and the Sea of Galilee. It was simply called, "The Abode of The Beloved." On the drive up, he had explained the basics of his faith community. He said, "We call ourselves 'Companions in The Spirit of Love.' We are an interfaith community of people. You know I am a Sufi and there are some liberal Sunni and Shiite Muslims too. Some are progressive Christians, some Liberal Jews, some Buddhists, some Hindus, some Taoists, some Jains, some Sikhs, some who call themselves 'spiritual, but not religious,' and we even have a few agnostics who feel comfortable breaking bread with us. The word 'companion' comes from the Latin and means 'with bread.' So before we eat, our blessing we share is a simple one: 'As companions we give thanks in the breaking and the sharing of this bread. In The Spirit of Love, Amen.' We live communally, eat a plant-based diet, shun weapons, and try to live lives of love. We celebrate many of the holy days of the great religions of the world. As you know tonight is the Jewish Passover and the meal is already prepared. Talk about synchronicity, Elijah!"

Habib parked the car and they were met by some companions with greetings of "Peace, Shalom, Salaam Aleichem, and Shanti." When they walked into the dining room they shared hugs and blessings of "Peace be with you" with everyone assembled. When Thomas and Miriam hugged the little one within jumped with joy prompting Q to exclaim the words from Ecclesiastes, "As thou knowest not what is the way of the Spirit, nor how the bones do grow in the womb of her that is with child, even thou knowest not the work of God who maketh all." John quickly joined in by bowing his head and whispering, "The Word is made flesh and dwells among us." Miriam was amazed and pondered these words in her heart.

They gathered around several large tables joined together to make one large square. The Companions found their places and showed their guests to their seats at the table. Habib went to the center seat of the head table and asked Elijah to stand beside him. With tears welling from his eyes he said, "Companions, for some 2,400 years our Jewish brothers and sisters have been celebrating their Passover from slavery and death. As we have done for years in keeping with Jewish tradition, we have always set aside a chair for the prophet Elijah and prayed for his return as prophesized in the Bible. My dear Companions, the scripture has been fulfilled! Elijah has returned! Elijah is here! Elijah has been given visions from God which he will share with the people of Earth. I am a partial witness to a small portion of those visions. We give thanks to GOD MOST HIGH that we have been asked to share in Elijah's safe return and in the mission of sharing his visions."

Habib reached for the unleavened bread and gave it to Elijah. Lifting it to the sky, Elijah simply said, "As Companions we give thanks in the breaking and the sharing of this bread. In the Spirit of Love. Amen." The community of Companions responded with "Amen" while the little one within Miriam gave a sweet and soft "amen" which reached the highest heaven.

GAIA'S GIFT

GAIA'S GIFT

The announcement read simply:

Earth Day Celebration
On the Beach at 4th street
6:15 – 7:30 AM
Bring a song, a prayer, a poem
or simply your presence
to share in a circle of love
as we celebrate the Earth.
You may also bring some slices of fruit
to be shared in a fruit salad.

The convener who posted the announcement around town and on the internet arrived well before dawn. She parked, gathered her items and walked to the beach. The rhythmic waves welcomed her. She sat on the sand, closed her eyes and welcomed the light. After a few minutes she placed a small sign behind her in the sand. It read: "Earth Day Celebration! Gather Here! Please observe silence until 6:30 AM! Thanks!"

geoagape

The waves waved to the celebrants as they arrived: families with small children, retired couples and singles, college students, and people who stopped by on their way to work. Upon reading the sign they too sat facing the dawning light. Fifteen minutes before sunrise the convener rose and faced the community of forty celebrants and quietly said, "We gather here as a community of love to celebrate the Earth. For the next twenty minutes, let's experience the sunrise in our own ways. Do whatever the Spirit of Love moves you to do: walk around, meditate, look for shells, hold hands, share smiles with one another and the Earth. We'll experience the sunrise alone and yet together. Once the sun has risen we'll gather in a semi-circle of love open to the rising sun and we'll share our offerings to the Earth."

Several sat still in the sand, but kept their eyes focused on the area where they knew the sun would soon rise. Some children went to the waves looking for sea shells. Dogs were left off their leashes, splashed in the surf, and chased several thrown balls. Softly, one woman began singing, "Good morning Earth, good morning sun, we're here to awake and have some fun." Several other people learned the tune and joined in a chorus.

More and more diffused light filled the horizon, brighter and more glorious with every passing second. Then, suddenly, a tiny sliver of light peered over the horizon and soon bursting forth in all of its glory, the full sun appeared. They smiled, laughed and some even danced.

The convener rose to face the gathered souls and said, "We give thanks for our Mother – Our Beautiful Earth! Now is the time to share your offerings of poems, of songs, of fruit, of dance, or any other gifts you want to share in this circle of love." A little girl of five said, "I have a poem to share. I wrote it myself – well most of it" as she looked up to her mother. She read the poem:

"I love my mother, she is so kind, she gives me things, even when I whine."

She looked again at her mother and said to the group, "she taught me that word to rhyme with kind." She then continued:

"I love the Earth, she is kind too.
She gives us good things, she's green, white, and blue.
Let's be good to our mothers – our moms and the Earth,
They have given us life, they have given us birth."

The little girl placed some banana slices in the bowl with the convener's peach slices, smiled and joyfully received the applause of the community.

An elderly man came forth and sang a hymn about the beauty of the Earth and placed some apple slices in the bowl.

A young couple came forth and announced, "We'd like to share an interpretive dance called 'The Gifts of Creation'." One by one, their movements gave symbolic expression: life crawling from the sea and then rising on two legs, the wonder of gathering and eating food, the joy of wading in the ocean, the act of physical love, the birth of a child, the caring of the frail, and finally the scattering of cremains back into the waters. As people applauded, the couple offered some mango slices to the common bowl.

An elderly woman with white hair came and announced her poem. "This poem is called 'NOW'."

babies birthing	bombs blasting	balls bouncing
lovers laughing	diseased dying	corpses cremating
grass greening	singers singing	teachers tasking
dogs digging	bees buzzing	parents punishing
killers killing	chickens clucking	moms mothering
sick sighing	waves waving	fathers fondling
hungry hurting	hawks hunting	cats climbing
fish flashing	parents praising	dolphins dodging
sun shining	moon moving	hawks hovering
worms wiggling	streams streaming	flowers flowering
children cuddling	rivers racing	gorillas grunting

cars careening	egos elevating	teens texting
leaders lagging	professors proffering	cooks cutting
Earth enchanting	Earth encircling	Earth expressing
Politicians puffing	Floods flowing	Spirit speaking

Quietly, she placed some sliced strawberries in the bowl, smiled, and said, "Elder exiting."

An African-American man of many years stepped forward and shared a great song about this wonderful world in the spirit of a great jazz musician.

After a few more offerings of poems, songs, and fruit the convener stood and stated, "I have some words to share in The Spirit of Love." She read the following:

GAIA'S GIFT

HOLY ONE, I lament for the Earth,
a wonderful mother, she has given us birth,
in a wonderful home of beauty and love,
blue, white, and green as seen from above.

I AM one with my Mother,
I now feel her pain,
she groans and she moans,
tears falling like rain.

Dare I speak for her now,
Like a prophet of old?
May my words speak forth her truth,
Loving yet bold.

I speak for our Mother, Gaia's her name.
Giving birth to formed love is the reason she came.
Seeing the planets where no life could take hold,
she said to herself, "I'll give warmth to the cold."

Creating a home in the grand Milky Way,
slowly life grew, day after day.
From tiniest cells to giants so deep,
she said to herself, "This promise I'll keep."

"Here I will now grow a garden so rare,
a garden of love, a garden of care,
a home where conscious love can take form,
where caring for others will always be norm."

geoagape

Her urge to create, to form love was sincere,
but others, less loving, said, "What have we here?"
They saw the marble of green, white, and blue
and said to themselves, "we'll create with her too."

So the Garden of Love was soon filled with weeds,
choking her delicate love-forming seeds.
Gaia knew a choice was at hand,
"Do I stay with my garden or do I fly from this land?"

As soon as she said it – she knew it was true,
she had skin in this game, there was nothing to do.
But to stay, tend her garden, loving all forms of life,
in the hope that one day, they'd choose love and not strife.

I celebrate Gaia, my love for her dear,
her beauty so wondrous, year after year.
Her seasons of change, her mountains so high,
her fish in the seas, her birds in the sky.

The care of a mother giving birth in a field,
giving love a new voice, increasing the yield.
Leaping lambs in the pasture, singing birds on the branch,
babes in the cradle, giving us a new chance.

To choose life, love, truth, hope, joy, and peace,
to choose happiness for all, to know it's within reach.

We are one with Gaia, why won't we see,
what happens to her, happens to me?
We are one with Gaia, why won't we see
what happens to you, happens to me?
We are one with each other, one life fills us all,
wherever we are on this terrestrial ball.

Spirit Speaks

The grandest gift Gaia can give,
is to show how to be, teach how to live,
sharing with others throughout all the day,
this is her truth, this is her way.

I speak forth for Gaia, hear my words, heed my plea,
I have her message to share, this is from she.

I AM your climate, changing faster each year.
Your concern is now just, you have reason to fear.
Bigger storms, longer droughts, falling lakes, rising seas,
losing your butterflies, frogs, trees, and bees.

I AM your fish swimming free in the sea,
Until huge nets drag us up, not letting us be.
You gorge on our flesh, giving no thought,
to the life that was lost with the money you bought.
In the days ahead when our schools do not run,
you will say to yourselves, "What have we done?"

I AM your animals in huge factory farms,
concentrated feeding brings concentrated harms.
Born to be fattened, tortured, and killed –
These are not the values I have instilled.

I AM your chickens seeing no light of day,
Hens' beaks all cut off, male chicks thrown away.
Eggs stolen from mothers, mourning their lost.
"Must make a profit, keep down the cost."

I AM your male calf, raised to be veal.
How can this be? Is this really real?
You chain and you feed, so my meat is so tender,
to consume my pink flesh your soul you will render.

geoagape

I AM the ever pregnant cow,
giving you milk so your taste buds say "Wow."
After my production falls and my efficiency run,
I'm off to be slaughtered, wind up on your bun.

I AM your dogs, I AM your cats,
you kill and you eat us, you even eat rats!
When will you learn, when will you see,
they have souls as you do, they need to be free?

I AM the ground under your feet,
once it was good, once it was sweet,
Now you fill it with trash, you fill it with shit,
So thoughtless, my children, I'm so tired of it.

I AM your water, once pure and so bright,
You could drink from a stream, oh a delight!
Now to drink it again, filter you must,
to remove all the filth, crust after crust.

I AM the air, once crystal clear,
Oxygen replenished year after year.
Now the sky is so black, some wear a mask.
You must clean it up, this is your task.

I AM the wind, blown to and fro,
within is my Spirit, this you must know:
Love is our purpose, love is our task.
Love one another, simply I ask.

You celebrate Earth Day, once every year.
It's the twenty-second day of April, I hear.
Many gather to celebrate life on our Earth,
renewing our covenant, giving some a rebirth.

Spirit Speaks

Dancers, musicians, and clowns fill the street,
sellers and buyers of Earth on their feet.
It's a wonderful festival, joy fills the air,
But I now ask you why, there's only one day to care?

For forty plus years now my prophets have spoke,
but many don't hear, some get lost in their toke.
Some hear the words of turmoil and doom,
retire to their homes, hearts heavy with gloom.

Some try to change their lives to be green.
Some just give up, hoping not to be seen.
Some say, "Climate change is just a big hoax!"
Some say, "The Earth will soon get rid of us folks!"

Celebrate Earth Day every day of the year!
Recycle, reuse, make your own beer!
May all who have breath and harm none freely live.
This is the message of Love that I give.

The future's still yours, the choice in your hands,
but you must now come together, throughout all the lands,
in harmonious unison you all must now give,
voice to my Voice, "Love all and let live!"

Say "We shall live love" together as one!
Say, "There's no need for greed under the sun."
If you all took only what's needed to be,
my Earth will provide every day you will see.

I must leave you now, but one last thing I will say,
tend my garden of love, please do this I pray.
May this wonderful planet, this beautiful ball,
be a garden of love, one house of prayer for us all.

The convener held her hands together in front of her heart, bowed and shared a "Namaste" with the community. She held up the bowl of gathered fruit and exclaimed, "We give you thanks, O Mother Earth, for this fruit you have shared with us. Coming from all over your wonderful creation we now combine it together as one giving thanks for our nourishment." Lowering the bowl, she smiled and said, "We give thanks for the blue skies and white clouds above us, the brown earth and the green of the fields and forests under and around us, and the blue water before us. We give thanks for the food from the Earth which nourishes us. We give thanks for this community of Love. May we carry this spirit of love into this new day. In The Spirit of Love, Amen."

The convener scooped out small portions of fruit into biodegradable bowls and the community tasted and agreed, "Hmmmm, it's so good!" After sharing the fruit, the convener smiled and said, "Group hug time." Everyone gathered close in a communal hug with abundant smiles and laughter.

One by one they left the circle of love to continue their new day.

A new day of hope,
    a new day of love for each other,
        and a new day of love for our Mother.

JOB'S DAUGHTER

PROLOGUE

There once was a woman in Abraham's land,
With neighbor and God, she walked hand-in-hand.
She had a daughter, a son, and a fine husband too;
good job, good health – she touched it, it grew.

Now one day came together in love,
The transcendent ones, in their home up above.
They gathered round God, singing sweet hymns of praise,
hearts full of joy, hands high they did raise.

Then into their midst, Satan he came,
but he was not singing, he had a new game.
"WHERE HAVE YOU BEEN?" God said with a sigh.
"Walking on Earth – in the sweet by and by."

"You allowed my siblings to create with a touch!
Big Bang, time and space, it grew – how so much!
They brought evolution and soon came new life,
but with it came trouble, horror, and strife!"

"From up here on high, do you know, will you see,
all of the pain, turmoil, doubt, woe, misery?
Yes, there is beauty and love this is true,
but allowing creation, it's all back on you."

"MY CHILD, WHAT YOU SAY, ALL OF IT'S TRUE,
BUT WHY DO SUFFERING AND DEATH BRING SO MUCH TROUBLE TO YOU?
MATERIAL LIFE BRINGS WITH IT THE GOOD AND THE BAD.
I'VE TOLD YOU ALL THIS; THIS CONVERSATION WE HAD."

"BUT THEY HAD TO CREATE, TO INVENT, TO EXPLORE,
THEIR OPTIONS UNLIMITED, THEY ALL WANTED MORE.
I ALLOWED THIS TO HAPPEN, YES THAT IS TRUE.
WITH LOVE IN MY HEART, WHAT ELSE COULD I DO?"

"HAVE YOU CONSIDERED MY SERVANT, JOBAT IS HER NAME.
THE WAY SHE LOVES LIFE, SHE'S IN MY HALL OF FAME.
IN SPITE OF SOME PAIN, SHE KNOWS WHAT TO DO.
LOOK HOW SHE LOVES, SO PURE AND SO TRUE."

"Yes, she loves now, with no questions, no doubt.
But she's safe in their hedge – now, take it out!
Remove it, and soon you will see,
She'll soon curse this life you allowed her to be."

"THE HEDGE THEY'LL REMOVE, MANY LIVES WILL BE LOST.
TO PROVE LOVE IS REAL, OH WHAT A COST!
THE DEATHS OF JOBAT AND HER CHILDREN WILL SHOW,
SPIRIT RISES FROM DEATH, THIS ALL WILL NOW KNOW."

Spirit Speaks

The Creator Ones all gathered around.
What would they learn, what would be found?
Was their creation worth all the pain that would come,
to Jobat and her family – to all, not to some?

To all that had been, both tall and to small,
on this beautiful planet, this terrestrial ball.
To all that had been by DNA made,
one cell to many, life's bold, big parade!

Life feeding on life, for what purpose, what ends?
To grow some more love? God and Satan made friends?
One more question to ponder - did we begin with a whim?
It's time for the show! Let God's play begin!

DAY ONE

Joby opened her eyes and wondered what the new day would bring. Her bald head reflected the new day's light. She prayed a quick prayer of thanks for another day of life, "Todah, raba, Adonai Elohim," but she knew her days were numbered. Day by day she felt her life slipping away. She was a spiritual Jew who loved many of the stories and values of her scriptures, but she gave herself permission to not accept everything written in The Tanak as God's Holy Word. She knew that her God of Love would never command as written in Deuteronomy 28:22 that a woman who had been raped had to marry her rapist. But she also knew that loving God and loving her neighbor were very important values in her life. She had learned this young in life from a liberal rabbi who once told her with a smile, "Joby, not all of the biblical stories are literally true, but there's so much wonderful truth in many of the stories! It's like being in a cafeteria; you have the joy and the responsibility of picking and choosing what goes on your plate! Just make sure you are guided by Love!"

Her husband Jacob became a secular Jew after their two children, Samuel and Deborah, were killed in the tragic accident two years before. They had attended a youth group meeting at their synagogue and failed to see and hear the approaching truck because of the unusually strong rain and wind. They, their two friends in the car, and the driver were all killed instantly. At their funerals, one member of the synagogue said to Jacob as he stood in the receiving line, "It was God's will. You must believe God has a reason for their deaths!" After a few weeks of mourning, Jacob in his grief had said, "I can't believe in a god who would allow our children to both be taken away so horribly! At least God could have spared one of them! If God is so powerful and all knowing, as people say, he could have prevented the accident! Just a few seconds earlier or later on that road and they'd still be alive! People who keep telling us it was God's will or God moves in mysterious ways can go to hell. Job's wife was right! We should all just curse God and die!"

Jacob came into Joby's room with her breakfast tray and her morning pills, smiled at her, kissed her on her forehead, her cheeks, and then on her lips. He said, "How's my bride this morning?" "I'm good! How's my sweetie?" Joby replied. "I'm okay, but I had a night of unsettling dreams. Is it okay to share them with you? You said we all need to be open and honest with each other as we go through this process!" Jacob said. Joby nodded her head, smiled again at Jacob and held his hand. "I dreamt we were on a walk and we discovered a cave. You turned on your cellphone light and immediately entered the cave leaving me outside. I called and called, but you never answered. I didn't have a light to go into the dark cave. I just stood there crying," Jacob wept while Joby reached out and hugged him. "It's okay Jacob. I'm still here. I'm not in the cave yet," Joby soothed. "Then I had another dream where you and I were riding on the back of two big, beautiful swans. We were doing acrobats in the air. We were laughing and having such a good time, but then all of a sudden your swan started rising higher and higher into the sky and eventually I couldn't see you anymore. My swan wouldn't follow after your swan. I tried to make him follow, but he wouldn't listen to me," said Jacob through some more tears. Joby said through tears of her own now, "It's okay. I'm still here. Those dreams are getting us ready for when I'll leave this earth. It's good we're feeling these feelings and having these talks! Disappearing into a cave and rising on the back of a swan into the sky! Freud and Joseph Campbell would love your dreams Jacob! Spirit is helping us prepare for our transitions – me rising into the spiritual realm and you making a new life without me here on Earth." Jacob got up from the bed and said, "Spirit should help you get better. Spirit should have saved our children. You still believe in angels! Where were their guardian angels? Sleeping, on vacation, watching the latest re-run on the big screen up high, or just standing by?" Jacob retorted. "I need to go to the store! Your mom will be here soon," Jacob said as he left the room.

Joby watched him leave the room and regretfully repeated her biggest question as she thought to herself, "Indeed, where were their guardian angels?" She believed their angels guided their souls to heaven, but she had also heard of so many stories of angels helping people survive terrible emergencies and so many stories of people experiencing miracles. "Why does God allow some to die and some to live?" she wondered.

Joby fell into a soft sleep and was awakened by some quiet footsteps she knew as her mother's. After smiling and sharing a big hug, her mother Anna said, "How's my girl?" "Okay mom. Thanks for coming. Mom, I've been thinking about my life, about Spirit, and about life in general. I need to talk out loud. Can you listen to me and not judge me too quickly?" Joby asked. "Sure, honey, let it go," Anna replied. Joby softly said, "Dad and Jacob aren't believers. I remember dad once saying, 'All that matters is matter.' Jacob used to repeat a phrase which one of his teachers said, 'you cease breathing and then you corpse' in difficult situations before Samuel and Deborah died and I got sick. You and I believe that isn't true and there are some who say they <u>know</u> it's not true. For us Spirit is more real than this material realm. There's more to us, than meets the eyes. Mom, I need to ask some questions and I've decided I need to talk with anyone who will listen in the hope that they will have some answers. Mom, there's so much pain, suffering, disease, death, and plain old evil in this world? I have three questions I need to ask and get answers to. Who created this world? Why was it created? How can all of the suffering on Earth be justified? Don't get me wrong, mom, I believe Spirit and Love are more powerful than death, but I need to ask these questions before I move on. Do you understand what I'm saying mom?' Joby implored.

"Yes dear, we all have these questions. We named you well Jobat – daughter of Job. Your father wanted to be original and I went along. Three questions: Who, why, and how can suffering be justified? Honey, I'm a simple woman. I believe what I was taught. God created the world. God's Spirit was consciously present helping things along to create the conditions for material life as we know it. Why? Maybe God got lonely! Maybe God wanted experiences, to be creative. Maybe creation is God's painting on the canvas of matter. Maybe creation is God's great musical overture with every material thing as the separate notes. You are right, there's a lot of suffering. Some say suffering makes us stronger. Stronger for what? Some say it's a test to show God we really love God. But if God is all knowing, why would God need proof? Honey, I just don't know. All I really know right now is I love you with all of my heart and you having this damn terminal brain cancer really makes me sad and I, … I, … I, …" Anna said as she began sobbing.

"I love you too, mom. Thanks for sharing your wisdom. I'm sorry I made you cry. Come here mom." Anna crawled into her daughter's bed and they took turns drying each other's tears with their kisses. Jacob found them sleeping, nestled together like a biblical hen and her chick when he returned from the store.

DAY THREE

The door-bell rang and Anna quickly answered it. After her talk with Joby, they decided it was time to ask the hospice staff if they could arrange for a "liberal" chaplain who was open to tough spiritual questions to meet with them. "Hello, I'm Chaplain Theo. I'm here to meet Joby and you might be Anna, Joby's mother?" Theo said. Anna replied, "Yes, I'm her mother. She's looking forward to your visit. I need to warn you. She's been asking some difficult spiritual questions the last two days. We asked for a liberal chaplain, one who can really listen to her and respond to her with love and not judgment. I trust you are like that?" Theo laughed and said, "I tell everyone if liberal is here, as he stretched his left hand left, and conservative is here, as he stretched his right hand right, then I'm over here, as he leaned way over to his left." Anna laughed and said, "Great, you are just the chaplain we need then. I'm afraid she's really living up to her namesake of being Jobat - Job's daughter. When we named her we wanted to be original and we created a girl's name in honor of a wonderful uncle of mine named Job. Her nickname Joby came very quickly after she was born." "That's okay, I've been doing this for over twenty years now and I've heard it all. In fact, I think it's great for Joby to be questioning. I'd much rather have her soul be engaged in living, than it allow a depressed personality to dampen her spirit," Theo replied.

They walked down the hallway and into the back family room which had been prepared for Joby's hospital bed and sitting area. Anna said as they entered, "Joby, this is Chaplain Theo, your hospice chaplain. Chaplain Theo, this is my beloved daughter Joby." "Please call me Theo. We need no formality here," Theo stated. "I'm going to leave you two to talk," Anna said as she left the room.

"Your mother said you've been asking some difficult questions, but she didn't say what they were. I've read through your files and please know my sympathy is with you for the loss of your children in that terrible accident. Your medical records state you have only a month or two, maybe a few more, of expected life unless there is a miracle. It appears the kind of tumor you have will allow you to live fairly normally until the last few days. So far the medicine is keeping the pain under control and that's a blessing. I understand the medical marijuana has been a blessing in that area. Joby, I'm here to be with you as much as you want and as much as I can be given my other commitments. I'm here to be with you through your last few days and provide you with whatever spiritual support you may need. I'm a great listener and I love a good discussion, so I'm going to stop talking and I'm ready when you are," Theo said.

Joby responded, "Wow, mom has a big mouth doesn't she! Seriously, thanks for your kind words about my children. It's been really tough without them. I always wondered how a mother got over the loss of a child; I never thought I would have to go through losing both of my children at the same time. Thanks for understanding my medical situation. You mentioned the possibility of a miracle. Well, I'm not looking for one. If it happens great, but right now I'm focusing on preparing to make my transition from this life to the next. But my mother is right. I do have a lot of questions and I don't have time for small, busy talk. So yeah, I have three big questions: Who is responsible for creating this world which has so much beauty, love and joy, but also has so much ugliness, hate, disease, death, and evil? Why did they create it? How can all the negative stuff I mentioned be justified if God is the Creator and is thought of as All Good?"

Theo laughed and said, "Well I'm the right chaplain for you to ask these questions. I'm going to tell you my full name. It's Theo D. Cey. My father was a philosophy teacher who specialized in the philosophy of religion. One of its biggest areas of discussion is the question of theodicy – literally, the justice of God. It's as you said – how can God be good and allow evil? Get it, my name is Theo D. Cey. He thought with the family name of Cey they could be creative and cute with my name. Dad and mom were both flower children from the 60s before they immigrated. I kinda like it! I've also done a lot of studying on the issue, being my name and all. Wow, Joby, we have a chance to really explore this issue if you really want to do so. I think it will help you in your transition. I believe it is okay to ask the questions you are asking. Do you know much about the book of Job?" Joby smiled and replied, "I read it several times throughout the years: once in my bat mitzvah training, once for a religion class in college, and once after my children were taken from me in the car accident. But I could never really agree with what I thought it was saying. According to my humble understanding, God allowed Job's children and his possessions to be taken away because God wanted to prove to Satan that Job would not curse him and want to die. Job has all these questions and then he gets brow beaten by God into silent submissison. At the end, it seems like God is sorry for what has been done to Job and he gets twice his former possessions back and new children. But what about the children who were killed by Satan? They seem to be just pawns in the divine wager. To me that was never right. Proving Satan wrong does not justify God's wager and actions in my opinion."

"Wonderful, you do know it! I have a suggestion. Let's read it again and pick out points for discussion. While we have The Bible in our hands, we may find some other passages that may help us. May I ask you some personal questions about your faith and your state of heart and mind and spirit?" Theo asked. "Sure I'm really enjoying our conversation so far," Joby replied. "Your record indicates you are a "Spiritual Jew" and not any of the regular Jewish group designations. So may I assume that you'd be open to answers to your three questions you have from different spiritual perspectives? Like you I'm liberal and I have many friends who are in different religions. Would you want me to ask them if they're willing to meet and talk with you too? Knowing them as I do, I believe they'd love to share some spiritual time with you," Theo stated. Joby exclaimed, "I'd love that. Sitting here in bed or in that chair gets boring very quickly. Send them in! But tell them Job's daughter is ready to wrestle!"

"Do you meditate Joby?" Theo asked. "I just pray. I've never done any intentional meditation," Joby replied. "One of the Psalms, I think it's Psalm 46, says, 'Be still and know I am God.' Would you like to meditate with me now? I can teach you a simple meditation and then you can meditate whenever you want," Theo stated. "Okay, I've always thought about meditating, but never got around to it. Funny how being terminally ill helps us choose priorities! What do I do?" Joby asked. "Let's see. Since you're Jewish I'm going to suggest we do a meditation related to your tradition. Many Jewish mystics practiced what's called Merkabah mysticism; Merkabah means chariot. Remember Elijah's chariot of fire and how the Bible says he was carried into the heavens? Well, Spirit's suggesting to me to ask you not to see yourself in a chariot but to think of an image where you are being carried into the heavens. See your soul being carried higher and higher into the highest realms of Spirit," Theo suggested. "That's easy! My husband Jacob just had a dream several days ago and we were riding on swans and my swan rose away from his. So all you want me to do is be still and see my soul on the back of a rising swan. I can do that," Joby said.

"Hopefully, that's only the beginning. Allow your soul to rise and to experience what Spirit will blow your way. Who knows – you may even get some answers to your questions, or maybe even get new questions to ask. Ready to begin?" Theo asked. Joby and Theo closed their eyes. She quickly imagined herself seated on a beautiful white swan which quickly began rising into the sky. She quickly realized that she didn't have to hold on because there was an energy binding them together. For minutes she rose through the sky and she felt great peace, but suddenly a siren from the street interrupted her ascent and she quickly came back down to Earth. She exulted, "Theo, that was beautiful! So wonderful, so peaceful! I was riding on the back of a swan rising into the sky! Thanks I need to do more of that!" "You are welcome Joby. A swan! Beautiful! I need to leave soon. Do we have a plan? Read and discuss Job. Do your swan meditation. I'll send some fellow spiritual companions over to talk with you. Would you like to have a prayer before I leave?" Theo asked. "Please, Theo, I'd like that." Theo held Joby's hands in his hands and prayed: "Thou whose love knows no end. You know we come to you in our broken wholeness with questions, but loving hearts. May our meditations guide us to your Truth. May our souls be healed even though our bodies will both soon turn back into dust. We give you thanks for this time together. We pray in The Spirit of Love. Amen." Theo stopped holding Joby's hands and stepped away from the bed. He placed his hands together in front of his heart, bowed and said, "Shalom, Joby. It was so wonderful to meet you and have this time with you. I look forward to being with you again in the days ahead. May God's peace be with you." Joby placed her hands together in front of her heart and returned the greeting, "Shalom, Theo. It is well with my soul." She watched Theo leave and then turned to look out the window. After a few moments, she was startled by what appeared to be a large white feather floating slowly down. She laughed and wondered to herself if what she saw had been real or maybe just an afterglow of the medical marijuana she had just taken right before Theo's visit.

Swan Song One

That night Joby slept peacefully until 3 AM when she dreamt of a singing swan.

>"Come with me Joby, jump on for a ride.
>Onward, within – where there's nothing to hide.
>I hear you have questions – three that's for sure.
>Come and receive answers – wonder no more.
>
>You may call me Celeste, as I climb in the sky.
>Within you'll see wonders as we soar beyond high.
>You want the whole truth, you want to know why,
>Creation began in the blink of an eye.
>
>I'll help you find truth in your quest to know more.
>Who's on the hook for it all, who wrote the score?
>Where's God in this mess? You are not scared to ask!
>To help in your search, is now my sole task.

Joby awoke with a smile and treasured every word of Celeste's Song.

DAY SEVEN

Joby smiled as her mother introduced Rev. Eli Jones to her. Theo had wasted no time in arranging the three visits by his spiritual friends. "Joby it's good to meet you. Theo has said a lot about you and told me of your questions. How are you feeling today? Are you up to wrestling theologically with me?" Eli asked. "I'm feeling okay and I'm ready to begin," Joby stated. "Great! I'm happy to share with you my perspective. I'm what I would call a modern-day Christian. I live in the 21st century and I accept the scientific knowledge available to us today. So I accept the ideas of The Big Bang and its subsequent expansion. I also accept the idea of evolution. I call myself a theistic, process-creationist because I believe God works through all of that scientific stuff. I believe God started The Big Bang to get the material stuff in the universe cooking, so to speak, and is now creating with consciousness through evolution as a kind of processing tool. I believe God's Spirit is guiding it all! So, yes, I believe that God is The Creator of this wonderful universe!" Eli shared. Joby responded, "Sounds like you and my mother agree on the answer to my first question. I'll let her know."

Eli smiled and said, "You second question is Why did God create this universe? For me it's a simple answer! God wants us to know God and to love God! The answer to your third question as to how all of the negative stuff in the universe can be justified will take longer for me to explain."

"Your scripture says, 'God is Love,'" Joby stated. "If God is Love why does he allow so much negative stuff if God is omnipotent and omniscient? I've heard some say God can only be two out of the following three – all knowing, all powerful, and all good. I've just heard of the Zika virus, for example. Thousands of innocent little children are being born with small brains just because their mothers got bit by a mosquito. If God knows about it and could stop it, but doesn't how can God be all good? Why did God allow a creation to evolve where life has to feed on life? Insects laying their parasitic eggs in other living beings. It took fourteen billion years for us to get to this point. Think of all of the millions of mothers and children dying in childbirth because of their primitive conditions with no medical assistance. Think of all the suffering and dying from all of the terrible conditions in those billions of years. Think of all of the violent deaths of sentient beings between The Big Bang and now. Think of all the violence in space as Super Novas explode and Black Holes swallow galaxies. It blows my mind! My children taken in a horrible accident! Where were God's guardian angels hovering over my children?" Joby shared.

"Joby, I've heard people say we can't know light without darkness, we can't know joy without sorrow, and we can't know love without hate or apathy. We live in a dualistic realm. In order to choose the good, in order to choose love, we have to have a world of free will where decisions matter and have consequences. Ecclesiastes says 'there's a time for everything under the sun' and that has to be true! The universe, this Earth, is a place where our souls experience this dance of opposites and grow in love," Eli responded. "So is heaven a place where there's no darkness, sorrow, and hate? If so, how can we know light, joy, and love there?" Joby asked. "Sometimes I think God just got bored by being alone and said, 'I'm going to experiment and see what happens!' Maybe God didn't know what would happen. Maybe God doesn't know it all. Maybe God is like a divine scientist whose experiment got out of control and now it can't be contained. Sometimes I even wondered if the god who created this world is a young god who was high when he or she had a high school science experiment to create a world and this is the resulting project. We're just like little ants and pawns in God's spectator game" Joby said.

"I know, I know, I have to admit I've had these thought before, but I haven't been brave enough to share them with anyone. I'd be out of a job if my ministerial board knew some of my doubts, some of my questions. Joby, all of these questions can lead you down into the rabbit hole if you let these questions get to you. Pretty soon you don't know up from down. If you lose track of the North Star, so to speak, you get lost and begin to live life aimlessly," Eli said as he stared out the window. A few minutes of awkward silence followed. Eli then looked at Joby and said, "Joby, may I be frank, even though my name is Eli," he said with a laugh. "Okay, thanks! You are dying. Are you and God okay? What if you died today? Don't you worry all of your questions are building a wall between you and God? Maybe now is not the time to ask these questions. Maybe it's time to be like an innocent child and just trust God's ways. Maybe it's time to accept that God moves in mysterious ways and that The Spirit blows where it wills. Can't you just trust that a good God is in control and that God gives life and God takes it away. Don't you want to be at peace with God before you die?"

"Reverend Eli, this is my namesake's moment. Job knew his sin was not commensurate with his suffering. He was not afraid to demand an answer from God. Remember Forrest Gump? This is my Lt. Dan moment when he crawls in the crow's nest and challenges God to get it on. I need to ask these questions which are burning in my bones. If God is truly Love, I trust I will be okay. If God is like the father in the Christian parable of the prodigal son, then God will welcome me home," Joby stated. "But the prodigal son came to his senses and recognized the error of his ways. That enabled the father to accept his son back home," Eli said. "Well I believe that God allows souls to repent even after death. How could God be pure Love if we were eternally punished and rejected solely on our decisions made on this Earth in such a short time? How could a God of Love punish us for an eternity just because of a few earthly decisions made in the haste of time! You are saying I'm wrong to ask these questions! I can't accept it as a mystery. God has given me a brain with which to think, a heart to feel, a mouth to speak, and free will to judge the good and the bad. Right now, I can't call this world good. If God is the Creator, how can God be good? You believe God is all three – all powerful, all knowing, and all good at the same time. Right now Eli, I can't accept that," Joby said.

Rev. Eli and Joby sat in a strained silence for a few minutes. Finally, Eli said, "Joby, it was good to meet you. I feel it's time for me to leave. I'll be praying for you to be able to love God and all of this creation before you die because I believe you have to choose to love God and all of God's ways now, on this side of the veil. I want you to be able to live in peace with God in heaven. Can you join me in prayer?" "Thanks for coming and honestly sharing your beliefs. Let's just have a brief moment of silence before you leave," Joby replied. For a few seconds they bowed their heads and then Eli rose, nodded toward Joby and walked out of the room. Joby said to herself, "A time to ask questions and a time to put your hand over your mouth."

geoagape

Swan Song Two

That night, Celeste came and took Joby for a ride and sang this song to her:

"The Big Bang was real, evolution is true,
fourteen billion years from then until you.
Eli was right, divine will made it all,
but God just stood by, let the kids have the ball.

All of the suffering, evil, and dread,
It's all on them, and not on God's head.
God loves your heart, your soul, and your mind.
You are loving and caring, you are true, you are kind.

God's shoulders are broad, God can take what you ask.
Feel free to ask questions, for God it's no task.
Rest assured God is Love, know that is true.
You'll soon know Pure Peace – there's nothing to do.

DAY TEN

"Hi Joby," Theo said as he walked towards Joby's chair. Sitting down and holding her hands in his, he smiled and said, "Let's just share some moments of silence before we begin." Joby took some deep breaths, making sure to exhale through her mouth. With every breath, her calmness and serenity expanded. Theo said, "Eli shared with me how his visit went with you and he was honest. He told me that in his opinion he probably failed you. He said questions are okay, but he felt the timing of your questions, so close to your death may hurt your relationship with God. He's worried about your soul." Joby nodded her head and said, "He means well; I know he's speaking from a loving heart. But I also know I must continue to ask questions. Hey, I need to tell you about Celeste. You taught me to meditate on a swan's back and she's come to me twice in the middle of the night with some beautiful songs. Her name is Celeste. Here I wrote down her songs. Aren't they beautiful! Spirit's speaking to me through Celeste." Theo read the songs slowly with his smile getting broader and broader with every line. "That's fantastic, Joby! How do you feel about Celeste's words?" Theo asked. "She seems to be saying that

God allowed the divine children to create this world. God could have stopped it, but because of God giving the children free will and loving them no matter what they did – they were allowed to start all of this," Joby stated.

Theo responded, "I know some Hindus believe that creation was not caused by the Absolute Supreme God, which they call Brahman, but by Brahma, their Creator God. They believe Brahma came out of a lotus flower from Brahman's navel and started everything. They also believe that creation is sustained by a second emanation of Brahman called Vishnu. Finally, they have a third deity-form called Shiva who dances the dance of destruction, which is followed by another creation by Brahma. To Brahman, it's only a dream; some call it an illusion or 'maya.' Others call it God's 'lila' or play. So in their understanding the trinity of deity-forms is responsible for the world and everything in it. Brahman is off on a cloud watching from afar like a Deist deity. This view takes some of the responsibility for the nastiness of the world off of God's shoulders and yet the play appears to be performed for Brahman." Joby replied, "It doesn't matter what name you give God, Brahman or Yahweh, it seems it still comes back to my point that God is responsible for allowing it all to be even though God didn't create it." They sat in silence for a few moments.

Eventually, Theo said, "Celeste, that's a great name for a meditation swan! I have a feeling you and Celeste will have some more celestial rides and songs. Did you read anything in the book of Job since we've met?" "Yeah, I have some scriptures I picked out," Joby said as she searched for her notebook. "I'm just struck by all of Job's bitterness. Some refer to the 'patience of Job', but to me that indicates they really haven't read Job at all. Job never did curse God like Satan wanted him to do, but he came very close to doing so, in my humble opinion, when he said things like: 'I will not speak with restraint; I will give voice to the anguish of my spirit; I will complain in the bitterness of my soul' as in 7:11. Look at 10:18 which says, 'why did you let me come out of the womb? Better had I expired before any eye saw me, had I been as though I never was, had I been carried from the womb to the grave.' He didn't curse God, but he's cursing the life God gave him. That's real anguish! His children are all gone! His possessions are all gone! His friends are telling him it's because he broke the covenant and sin brings punishment. Job acknowledges he has sinned, but never agrees that he sinned in proportion to his so-called punishment. Take one child, but all of them?" Theo asked, "Joby I'm assuming you don't believe Job was a real person, correct?" "Of course not, it's a story. It's a great story. Like one of my teachers used to say, 'This story isn't true, but there's truth in this story.' The author of Job was wrestling with the question, 'Why do bad things happen to good people?' For some the traditional answer is given by Job's three friends – sin brings punishment because of the covenant. But we know Job's suffering was because of God's wager with Satan. That can't be true," Joby stated. "Joby, do you wish you had never been born like Job cries out?" Theo asked. "Of course not! I love my life, however short it will be. I love my family. I love my kids." Joby began to cry. "Damn it, they were here and then gone - too soon, too soon! They didn't have a chance to grow up, get married, make me a grandmother. I love rainbows, I hate cancer, I love seeing the dancing diamonds of light on the Sea of Galilee, but I hate the hurricanes and tsunamis that kill people. I hate war, but I love seeing people helping those in need. I love Jacob, I love him touching me. I'm going to die soon and I don't know why! Is there a why? Maybe Shakespeare was right it's just a lot of loud noise which doesn't mean a damn thing! Theo, I need to know, I want to laugh, I want to cry, I want to love, I want to make love, I want to live, I want to … ," Joby cried as her tears began falling from her eyes.

Theo rose and put a hand on her shoulder and allowed his tears to fall also. Then he said, "Remember what Celeste said, 'Rest assured, God is Love, know that is true, you'll soon know pure peace, there's nothing to do.'" They looked deeply into each other's souls, began laughing and then shared a powerful primal hug.

Theo said, "I need to leave soon. Would you like to pray with me before I leave?" "Yeah," Joby said as she wiped her eyes. Theo put Joby's hands on her heart and placed his right hand over them. He held his left hand above Joby's head as he prayed: "Thou, who cries with us. Thou who is pure Love. We come together in honest searching and caring. We love you and we love most of this life, but sometimes down here it gets confusing. So much pain, so much sorrow. We trust that you are Emmanuel – God with us. We trust that you know our hearts yearn for your Wisdom and for your Breath, your Spirit of new life. We give you thanks for the space to wander as we wonder, to question, to ask, to complain, to break down in tears, to be human. Remind us that your Spirit is within us and that we are never alone. Now hear our silent moans and groans. … In the Spirit of Love. Amen."

"You always end you prayer with the phrase 'In the Spirit of Love,'" Joby observed. Theo stated, "Yeah, there was a Sufi mystic who once asserted love was all he needed. Kind of like the Beatles, huh!" "So what are you?" Joby asked. "Joby, I'm just a Lover: I try to love God and my neighbor. I simply try to follow Love's Way. I guess that makes me a LovesWayer. I'm grateful that The Spirit of Love is my companion, my inspirer. I'm thankful there are others like me who just simply want to receive, celebrate, teach, and share Love. Picasso once did some paintings where he had a dove in the middle with people dancing around it. That's my religion, that's my spirituality." "That's really beautiful, Theo. Thanks for sharing that. You and I did some real dancing with The Spirit of Love today, didn't we?" "Yes, we did my sweet spirit companion! That we did! See you in a few days, unless you need me sooner. Shalom, Joby." "Shalom, my wonderful dancing partner in The Spirit of Love."

Swan Song Three

After Theo left, Joby took some pain medication and drifted off to sleep where Celeste soon greeted her with this song as they soared up into the sky:

> Joby, my dear, your tears now will dry,
> Look down below from our place way up high.
> The Earth in its beauty, blue, green, and white,
> The sun and the moon and their dazzling light.
>
> The beauty of mountains, valleys, and fields,
> Orchards bursting with fabulous yields,
> Birds, dolphins, pandas, emus, and bears,
> Eggs in their nests and young in their lairs.

All of a sudden a dark raven appeared by Celeste's side and sang another song:

> Joby, my dear, there is beauty it's true,
> But there's more now to be seen by Celeste and by you,
> In a few billion years, the sun and its light,
> Will all be gone in a dark frozen night.
>
> No flowers will bloom, no birds flying high.
> No dolphins at play in this sweet by-and-by.
> Between now and then, this is the truth.
> Life feeds on life, bloody claw, bloody tooth.
>
> Sentient beings in the pain throes of death,
> Claws at their throats, crying last breath.
> The weak that are caught, the young that are lost,
> Feed the young of the stronger, this is the cost.

See their suffering, their horror, feel their pain, hear their cries,
Soon rivers of tears will stream from your eyes.

Celeste shows you the good, the beauty - all true.
But here's one more question, I now ask of you.
What kind of a God has so much blood on its hands?
What kind of God gives to wolves baby lambs?

Joby abruptly awoke from the raven's song with a shivering shout. She took a deep breath and cried for Jacob who was sitting alongside her. "Celeste came and took me for another ride, but then a raven came and sang to me too, Jacob," Joby cried. "Wow, you really shouted loudly. You woke me. Pretty scary, huh," Jacob said. "How can life be so beautiful and so horrible at the same time?" Joby asked. Jacob hugged her and replied, "Honey, you know my answer, 'It is what it is.' We have to take the bad with the good. We're here today and gone … . Sorry, sweetie, I'm just a fool who needs to watch his mouth."

DAY FOURTEEN

As the doorbell rang Joby's heart raced a little faster. Theo had arranged for her to meet with a Buddhist monk. She had read a little about Buddhism, but she had little experience with it and had never met a real monk. Anna escorted him into Joby's room. He bowed and they exchanged the Namaste greeting. "Joby, this is Monk. That's how he introduced himself to me and wants to be known. "Peace and blessings to you Joby." "Peace and blessings to you Monk."

Monk smiled and said, "Rev. Theo says you need to talk about life and you have three questions. He also said you are doing a swan meditation. May we begin with some quiet time. You do your meditation and I will sit in meditation with you." "I'd love that," Joby replied. She closed her eyes. Very quickly Celeste showed up and she climbed on her back quickly rising into the air. Literally, in a blink of an eye, Joby could feel herself going into REM, rapid eye movement. Her eyes were moving quickly behind her closed eyes as a great peace of theta waves soothed her. Suddenly, she saw Monk flying beside her and Celeste. He smiled and said, "We're flying Joby! Isn't it grand! Where do you want to go?" Joby shouted, "Can I see my children?" Monk smiled and led Celeste into a bank of clouds and then settled into a valley with a beautiful lake. Monk said, "Samuel is here, but not Deoborah. We can't stay long." Joby jumped off of Celeste and quickly found Samuel sitting by the lake. Embracing each other Samuel said, "Mom you're here! Did you die too?" "Not yet Samuel, but soon. It's so wonderful to see you, hear you, touch you. I've missed you so much. You are here! Your spirit is alive! It's true, we live on! Where's Deborah?" Samuel replied, "We were together for a little while, but she quickly went back to Earth. Mom, she chose to be reincarnated as a Palestinian girl in Gaza." Joby looked at Monk who smiled and simply said, "Karma!" Samuel stated, "She's a much older soul than I am. I've been allowed to stay in between realms for a while until I decide I'm ready to go again." After sharing some more conversation, Monk smiled at Joby and pointed to the clouds. Thankful for the experience with Samuel, Joby hugged her son, climbed on Celeste and they flew away into the clouds.

Joby heard Monk whisper, "When you are ready you may open your eyes." "How long were we gone?" asked Joby. "Forty minutes of Earth time." "It was so beautiful." "Yes, it is." "Monk, was that real? Did I really just see my son?'" Monk smiled and said, "Your son is not just your son. You are not his only mother. There is no one personality. Souls have many incarnations, many personalities. When he is ready to lose his little self, his little identity of Samuel, then he will be ready to continue his reincarnation. Hopefully, his karma gets little and little until it's gone and he is the True Self. Your daughter whom you knew as Deborah has been born with a new name and a new family. She will grow, choose, and die, grow, choose, and die until the wheel is balanced."

"So what are your answers to my three questions?" Joby asked. Monk replied, "I have no answer to who created, who is responsible for creation - it just is. I have no answer to the question why – again, it just is." "Jacob would like that. Maybe he was a Buddhist in a previous life!" Joby stated. Monk just returned a knowing smile. Monk continued, "Buddha didn't care about answering these metaphysical questions. His whole focus was on how to free himself and others from this experience of suffering, this experience of being unbalanced. He gave us The Four Noble Truths and The Eightfold Path to help us. I am on that path. Joby, you are correct. This realm is full of dukkha, which means suffering that originates in experiencing the world being out of balance. Birth, life, death, birth, life, death, on and on, on and on. Buddha taught a way to be free, to be balanced in this realm and the next. He taught us that we can smile even as our bodies suffer. We come to know that we are not the suffering, but we also know we are not the smile. Ultimately, we will know a "time and space" where there is no time and space. We will know that there is no suffering and there is no smile. Only Nirvana! This world of suffering and our experience of it will be extinguished. It's beyond words, but we can get a foretaste of it here. Light! Love! Truth! Peace! Joy! Serenity! Surrender! Stillness! No Light! No Love! No Truth! No Peace! No Joy! No Serenity! No Surrender! No Stillness! Nada! Nada!"

"That sounds beautiful and mysterious at the same time Monk. Thank you. Thank you for taking me to be with Samuel. Thank you for sharing your time and your heart with me," Joby stated. "Joby, soon you will be released from this lifetime. Soon you will be reborn. You are an old soul too. You are close to The Pure Land. Know and grow! Know and grow! Know and grow! Peace and blessings to you and yours! May all beings be happy!" Monk replied. "Peace be with you Monk," Joby said as they shared a farewell Namaste.

A few hours later while watching the news on TV she saw there had been another round of military exchanges between some Palestinians shooting rockets from Gaza and responding Israeli forces. The news stated that over one hundred Palestinians and ten Israelis were killed in the fighting. Joby shook her head, cried, and quickly turned off the news as she wondered and worried about her little girl.

DAY SEVENTEEN

"Hi Joby! Monk said he enjoyed his time with you." "Theo, it was wonderful! Did he tell you what happened? We meditated and before I knew it I was hugging Samuel. It was so real! I hated to leave him, but I know I'll be seeing him again soon. What he said about my three questions makes sense and gives me some peace. I have to be honest, though, I still have to ask my questions of who, why, and how? Why is the Karmic Wheel wound so tight? Why did it have to start in the first place? Who started it? I'm not satisfied with 'It just is.' Someone has to be responsible!" "You are truly Job's daughter. Sounds like you're quoting Job 13:3, 'Indeed, I would speak to the Almighty; I insist on arguing with him.' Joby you question the goodness of God and the goodness of creation. Do we really know what is good and bad? There's a great Taoist story about a man whose son caught some wild horses. A neighbor celebrated the son's father with such good fortune, but the father said, 'Who knows what is good or bad?' The son broke some bones when he was trying to tame one of the horses and the neighbor said that was terrible. Again, the father said, 'Who knows what is good or bad?' A few weeks later an army came through the village and was drafting some men into the army to fight a terrible war. But the young son could not go because of his injuries." Joby replied, "Yes, I see that. Out of pain brought some safety from being hurt worse. Healing and growing can come from pain and suffering. Theo, I'm tired. My body has one foot in this world and one foot in the next. Guess what I saw on TV yesterday? I was watching a wild animal show. They showed a wildebeest mother giving birth to her baby. The mom was licking the baby as it quickly struggled to get to his feet and guess what happened. Fifteen minutes after it was born a pack of hyenas came. The mother was too far from the herd. She tried courageously to defend her baby, but there were too many. It was horrible! One hyena got the tail, another took hold of the head, several others got legs and it was ripped apart right in front of its mother's eyes who was still bellowing and kicking. Born to die! I know it was good for the hyenas and their young, but it was so horrible for the baby and its mother. How could a good God create that?"

Theo asked, "Joby, do you know the scripture which says that originally God gave humans and animals only the green plants of the fields for food and they didn't kill or eat each other for meat until after the flood?" "Theo, it's a nice story, but I don't believe that was ever true. I accept evolution and the survival of the fittest. I think whoever wrote Genesis was as uncomfortable with all of the bloody deaths as I am. I could believe that God wanted us humans to be vegans and to not eat flesh, but I don't believe the wild animals were ever vegans. Did mom tell you that ever since I've started asking these questions and getting in touch with this bloody creation, I've been eating a vegan diet? I was a vegetarian years ago in college after I watched some documentaries about factory farming and what flesh eating does to the environment, but it's so hard to do in this culture. Keep the family happy, right?" Theo replied, "Joby, I understand completely. I became vegan years ago for spiritual, health, and ecological reasons. Joby, I know you are Jewish, but can I share some research I've found concerning Jesus? Remember, he was born, lived, and died as a Jew!" Joby nodded her head affirmatively. Theo continued, "Recent research suggests that Jesus and his family were Nazoraeans and possibly Essenes who both were known to be primarily vegan. Eusebius quotes Hegesippus who says that Jesus' brother James 'was holy from his mother's womb' and that he never had strong drink 'nor did he eat flesh.' The research also suggests that they were against the Temple sacrifice of animals and that his cleansing of the Temple was primarily out of his compassion for the sacrificial animals. If that is true he would join a long line of Jewish prophets who spoke out against the Temple sacrifices. Jesus quoted them saying God wanted compassion and mercy for all beings in God's creation." Joby asserted, "That's a Jesus I could believe in. Theo, I'm not feeling well. Let's just sit still."

"Okay, Joby." They sat in silence for almost ten minutes. Eventually, Theo asked, "There's one more thing I'd like to teach you before I leave. For me it's one of the most beautiful scriptures. According to the Christian scriptures Jesus breathed The Holy Spirit upon the disciples. The Hebrew word for "spirit" is "ruach" which can also mean wind and breath. The Greek word "pneuma" also has the same three meanings. Scripture says he breathed on them and said, 'Receive the Holy Spirit.' So literally, in the Greek New Testament he is quoted as saying 'Receive the pneuma' as he 'pneumaed' on them. May I teach you another meditation I do related to this? Thanks! We'll use Jewish terminology. Be still. Now take some deep breaths. Now take some more deep breaths saying these words, 'Come Shekinah, Heavenly Dove, Breathing Light, Breathing Love.' Do that now for a few seconds. Now on your exhale, breath the Ruach to whomever you want saying these words and saying the person's or thing's name, 'Receive The Spirit of Love.' I send it to the universe, the Earth, my family, my foes, people in need of healing energy, and animals just to name some of the beings with which I share; I even send it to myself. Ready to try?"

Joby lay still in bed and drew in and breathed out several long breaths. Then she began sharing her breath, her spirit, her ruach - in The Spirit of Love. She shared it with her family, factory farm animals, wild animals, Palestinians, Israelis, Rev. Eli, Monk, Theo, and finally she blew some ruach in, through, and around her own body. Suddenly, she imagined the Earth from above and shared the Breath of Love with her. With another breath, Joby shared the Spirit of Love with the whole universe. With her last breath in the meditation Joby said out loud, 'Thou whose Spirit is my breath, Thou who has given me life, Receive back unto thyself your Spirit of Love.'" Joby opened her eyes and whispered, "Wow. That was beautiful! Thanks I needed that!" "You are welcome Joby. It's a modified form of what Monk and his fellow Buddhists would call Metta meditation. Joby, I'll assume our Spirit of Love meditation was our prayer." "Yup! Nothing more to say or do!" "Shalom, Joby! The Spirit of Love is with you!" Theo said as he blew some breath in her direction. Joby took a deep breath and blowing some exhalation in Theo's direction said, "And also with you."

DAY TWENTY FOUR

Joby was sitting in her chair by the window when Jacob walked in saying, "I had another dream last night. I need to talk about it with you" as he reached for her hand. Joby smiled and replied, "I hope it's better than the last dreams you shared with me. I don't like seeing you upset." "I dreamt I was in Gaza. I don't know how I got there or why I was there. I was walking the streets and looking at the conditions. How can so many people live so closely together like that? Anyways, I saw a group of children playing in the streets. I smiled at them and they smiled back at me. Then one of them, a little girl came over and …" Jacob said and started crying. "Joby, it was her! It was Deborah. She didn't look like Deborah, but I could see Deborah in her eyes and in her gestures. I told her, 'I had a daughter once who looked a lot like you' and then she said, 'Don't be silly daddy. I am Deborah in a new body.' We were laughing and hugging each other and then I woke up. It was so real Joby. She was so real. I don't know what to think, but I know how I feel."

Joby smiled, and cupping both of Jacob's hands in hers said, "What a gift you were given – we were given! I need to tell you about a meditation, or dream, or whatever it was I had a few days ago. Remember I talked about my visit with Monk the Buddhist? Well in my meditation with him, we flew on the backs of swans, I was on Celeste, and they took us to see Samuel. Jacob we hugged in my meditation just like you and Deborah hugged. Like your experience it was so real. I'm glad I didn't tell you about it because, oh, I'm getting goosebumps as I'm telling you this. Jacob, I asked Samuel if Deborah was here and he said, 'No, she chose to reincarnate again.' Jacob, sit down! Jacob he told me that she was reborn in Palestine as a girl. My meditation and your dream seem to confirm that life goes on. At least it confirms that The Spirit of Love is moving in mysterious ways! The soul essence of the one we knew as Deborah is now living, growing, learning, and loving in that little Palestinian girl body." "Maybe you are right; maybe we aren't just rotting corpses after we die! What did Samuel look like? Did he say anything for me?" Jacob asked. Joby laughed and related, "He said he was looking forward to joining you in another lifetime, but this time he was going to be the father!" Jacob kissed Joby and said, "Beautiful woman, love of my life, I love you now and forevermore. You've been so good to me. You've been so good for me. I miss you, I miss what we had. I miss touching you and you touching me." "I miss it too Jacob. We shared a lot of bodily fluids, didn't we! Oh to be young again. Jacob we need to focus on the blessings we had, the blessings we have now, and the blessings we'll have in our lives to come," Joby said calmly. "In a few days my body will return to dust, but my spirit will birth back into the spiritual realm. Eventually, I have a feeling we'll find each other again." They kissed while a gentle breeze blew in from the open window.

"Jacob, Spirit gave you and me a real gift. There's a scripture I want to share with you. Give me the Tanak. Thanks! Here I found it! Job 33:15 reads, 'In a dream, a night vision, when a deep sleep falls on people. While they slumber on their beds, then he opens peoples' understanding.' Jacob, give thanks for that scripture has become true for you! What a blessing! Thank you wonderful Spirit of Love!"

DAY THIRTY ONE

The brain tumor must have grown, because Joby was now experiencing more pain and couldn't walk. With the increased pain came increased medication which helped her to sleep more. Theo had called the day before and asked Joby if she wanted to meet another chaplain friend of his, this time a Jewish rabbi and Joby agreed.

Rabbi Joshua entered Joby's room while she was sleeping, sat by her bed, and prayed. A few minutes later, Joby opened her eyes and said, "Shalom, rabbi." "Shalom, Joby. May I tell you what I see as I read your energy field? Thank you for allowing me to do so. I think you'll like what I'm seeing. I can see part of you is here on this bed and another part is flying high! Your chakras are amazingly open and active even with the cancer. Your color is good. I see a lot of gold, purple and a beautiful white glow in your field. Ah, your son Samuel is close by. He's ready when you are ready to cut the spiritual cord to your body. There's a beautiful swan hovering. She says her name is Celeste. What fun you've had. Oh, there's a raven too. Not so much fun, but he says he's only doing his job. Joby, your cord is thin. You have just a few days left. What would you like to do? Pray in silence? Pray together? Talk about your three questions or are we beyond that? Your choice, Joby." "I want to hear your quick – in a nutshell – answers to my three questions. I don't need nor do I feel up to your dissertation answers. Who? Why? How can it be justified?" Joby responded.

"Joby, I'm an extremely liberal Jew. Our Orthodox friends even say I'm not a real Jew, because of what I do and don't accept as part of the real Jewish Way. Who? My answer, simply put, is to suggest the idea of a Demiurge, a secondary maker, is as close to the Truth as we can get here on this Earth. Plato and the Gnostics say a good, loving, perfect, spiritual God would not have created this material world full of so much pain and suffering and I agree. The GOD with which I am in relationship is Spirit and Love. I think it may have all started when GOD who was THE ONE, an undifferentiated unity said to GODSELF, 'I AM, AND I AM LOVE, BUT LOVE TO BE REAL NEEDS AN OTHER.' So GOD manifested out of GODSELF secondary beings whom GOD loved deeply. As PURE LOVING SPIRIT, GOD stays within the Realm of Love. It's always there for us when our love becomes pure enough to enter and join in the ONE LOVE SHARED BY MANY. We can get a foretaste of that love here, but it's only a foretaste. Why did the Demiurge create this material world? It wanted to create, it needed to explore. It felt divine power wanted to express itself. Schopenhauer called it 'The Will.' He was wrong about it being blind, however. The Will, The Power, whatever you want to call it is conscious and knows what it is doing. Think about this miraculous world. Think about how life began from single cells, DNA with the chromosones, ACGT, protons, neutrons, quarks, anti-quarks! The Demiurge is quite a designer. It doesn't allow itself to feel the pain and suffering the beings of life feel. Like an objective scientist in their lab experimenting on animals, the Demiurge feels its need to explore what can be outweighs the suffering. How can it be justified? Ultimately, it all goes back to GOD doesn't it? GOD allows it because of GOD'S love for the Demiurge and the other secondary helpers. GOD also loves the creation, the good and the bad. I believe GOD experiences it all and yet is somehow removed from it all at the same time. It's a panentheistic view. I know it doesn't make any rational sense, but it's my best answer. Out of GOD'S Loving heart, and everything I've said is just a metaphor you understand, come beings into this material realm who live and teach the way to live in this realm so they can find their way back home to the spiritual realm of Love and Light. Joby I believe in reincarnation. Sometimes I ask how can a loving GOD allow us to have to come back again and again until we grow enough in love. Why can't we just go home and not have to feel the pain again and again? I know people say it's karma or we need to grow in love, but I get impatient with 'the divine order' just like you are impatient."

"Joby, we're caught up in a game of life which was created by the Demiurge and its helpers. It's their creation, their sustaining, their destruction, their play of time and space if you will. We're tiny sparks of Love and Light that got caught up in this creation. Maybe when The Big Bang happened that's when our soul-sparks were cast into the material realm. Maybe we don't have to come back, but we choose to come back like bodhisattvas who forego full Nirvana until all beings have reached enlightenment. Our Love keeps us here to help others know and grow love. Ultimately, my dear one, please understand that everything I've said may be just pure nonsense."

"Joby, I can see your physical body is tired and needs to rest. May we pray together? Close your eyes and may our souls come together in The Spirit of Love." They closed their eyes. Again, it was just like being with Monk; Joby's eyes started shaking in rapid eye movements and she quickly entered Theta brainwave state. Celeste appeared and they rose into the sky, higher and higher.

Finally, Celeste landed on a beautiful cloud. Joby walked through some billowy curtain-like clouds and entered a place of surreal beauty. Joshua was waiting for her. Without saying any spoken words, they communicated. "Isn't this so wondrously grand! I come here as often as I can. Words just can't do it justice! It's so peaceful here. No pain. No suffering. Well, I shouldn't say none because there's just an iota of suffering in knowing that back on Earth and the other material platforms there's so many beings who are suffering and need some love in their lives. See those souls over there? They have chosen to stay here for now. See those clouds up there? That's a realm that's closer to the heart of GOD, but I'm not at liberty to share it with you now. One has to grow into it." Joby asked, "But why do I have to grow into it? Why does God put up a boundary around the heart of God?" Joshua replied, "It's not a boundary Joby. GOD is everywhere and nowhere at the same time. I'm sure you've seen the letters 'GODISNOWHERE' before. What do they say? Some read, 'God is no-where' while others read 'God is now-here.' Both are true at the same time. GOD is nothing: GOD is no-thing. No boundaries. No place. No time. GOD IS or better yet, GOD AM. Joby you are a great soul. You have loved well. You have a lot more love to share." Joshua was quiet and then said, "Even though there is no time here, back on Earth it is time for us to open our eyes and return to our bodies. Awake as you will." Joby opened her eyes and shared a smile with Joshua. "Any more questions?" he asked. Joby shook her head and then asked, "Will I see you again? Why do I feel like I've known you forever?" Joshua responded, "Joby, receive, celebrate, and share God's Love and remember wherever Love is, I AM." "Joshua, I love you." "And I love you, precious one. Shalom, my beloved companion." "Shalom, Joshua."

He rose, kissed Joby on her forehead, raised his right hand upwards to the sky and placed his left hand above Joby's heart saying, "Shalom, Joby, receive The Spirit of Love" and blew a long breath over the length of Joby's body. Joby felt a warm energy bathe her entire body and she knew she was whole even though the tumor remained and would soon end her current incarnation.

"Shalom, Jobat, daughter of Job." "Shalom, Joshua." "The Spirit of Love is with you Joby, until we meet again!" "And also with you dear Joshua!" Joby closed her eyes into a restful sleep.

DAY THIRTY EIGHT

Theo walked into Joby's room. Her family had all gathered around her for her last few days. For the past week, she had been peacefully resting, opening her eyes for only a few short words now and then. Theo hugged Anna and then Jacob who said, "I want to thank you for being with Joby these last two months and for asking the other chaplains to visit. Those visits have helped Joby immensely. She's at peace and her peace has given us strength and peace. I can't thank you enough." Theo responded, "Thank you Jacob. I'm glad we could help. It was a privilege to meet and be with Joby and you. She has shown us how to live and now she's showing us how to die." Jacob asked, "Who was that rabbi Joshua? From Joby's words about him he's not like any rabbi I've ever known." Theo smiled and said quietly, "He's a modern day Essene and lives in an ashram with some companions at the foot of Mt. Carmel. They are a wonderful spiritual community of Love and I retreat there as often as I can." Joby awoke and said, "Theo is that you?" "Yes, I'm here Joby." "Theo, thank you. You and your friends have given me so much." "You are welcome dear." "I'm not long for this Earth." "I know dear one and soon you will be free to soar with your angels and loved ones." "I have been soaring these last few days, in and out, up and down, in and out. It's so beautiful over there!" "Joby, is there anything more I can do for you?" "Come closer. Closer! Closer!" Joby took a deep breath and breathing on Theo whispered, "Receive The Spirit of Love." With tears of joy, Theo returned his breath of blessing, "Receive The Spirit of Love." Joby said quietly to her friend, "Spirit says come back in two days. Same time." "I'll be here my friend."

That evening, just before midnight, Joby heard a still, small voice from within: "JOBY, MY BELOVED! JOBY, MY BELOVED! JOBY, MY BELOVED!" Joby shivered and responded, "Beloved, you bless me with your soothing sound. But I'm surprised! There's no bombastic, bellowing, boasting, bloviation with which you challenged Job?" "YOU TRULY ARE JOB'S DAUGHTER! THAT WAS HOW THE AUTHOR OF JOB PORTRAYED ME! SHE WAS QUITE THE DRAMATIST, WASN'T SHE? ARE YOU READY FOR ANSWERS TO YOUR THREE QUESTIONS? ONE WORD ANSWERS THEM ALL! YOU ALREADY KNOW IT! LOVE! CREATION WAS CREATED FROM LOVE, FOR LOVE AND IS JUSTIFIED BY LOVE. THERE WAS A 'TIME' BEFORE THERE WAS TIME WHEN 'I' WAS ALL THERE WAS. I LOVED MYSELF, BUT I KNEW THERE WAS MORE. OUT OF MYSELF CAME MY CHILDREN. I LOVE THEM DEARLY! THEY WANTED TO CREATE A MATERIAL REALM. THEY SAID, 'MATTER MUST MATTER AND MATTER WILL MATTER, IT WILL MAKE A DIFFERENCE!' WHAT A DIFFERENCE! YOU ARE RIGHT. THEIR CREATION IS FULL OF BEAUTY AND ALSO FULL OF HORRIBLE SUFFERING. I AM CONSCIOUS OF IT ALL. I ALLOWED THE BIG BANG, BUT I INFUSED INTO EVERY ENERGETIC MANIFESTATION THE TINIEST OF SPIRITUAL SPARKS. YOUR SCIENTISTS WILL SOON REALIZE THE SPIRITUAL BASIS OF THEIR SEARCHED FOR UNIFIED THEORY. MY MYSTICS HAVE BEEN GIVING THEM HINTS FOR THOUSANDS OF YEARS. MY INCLUSIVE SPIRIT IS THE CANVAS ON WHICH THE MATERIAL WORLD EXPRESSES ITSELF!

WHAT A PAINTING! WHAT A PLAY! I'M SORRY FOR THE LOSS OF YOUR CHILDREN IN YOUR CURRENT INCARNATION! I'M SORRY FOR THE PAIN WITH YOUR TUMOR. BUT ASK YOURSELF, 'WOULD YOU HAVE MET ELI, MONK, JOSHUA, AND THEO WITHOUT IT? WOULD YOU BE THE PERSON YOU ARE NOW WITHOUT YOUR PAIN AND SUFFERING?"

"JOBY THE BIG QUESTION I ASK MYSELF IS, 'WOULD I ALLOW EVERYTHING TO HAPPEN AGAIN IF I HAD THE CHOICE?' THINK OF IT JOBY, NO PAIN BUT NO RAINBOWS. NO SUFFERING BUT NO JOY OF GIVING BIRTH. NO DEATH BUT NO RAPTURE OF ORGASMIC BLISS. NO BLOOD ON THE GROUND BUT NO DOVE GLIDING ON THE WIND. WOULD I DO IT AGAIN? WOULD I ALLOW IT AGAIN, KNOWING WHAT I KNOW NOW? JOBY DO YOU UNDERSTAND YOU ARE SPIRIT OF MY SPIRIT, BREATH OF MY BREATH, YOU ARE LOVE OF MY LOVE? WOULD I DO IT AGAIN? A TROUBLING QUESTION IT IS! I HAVE A SUGGESTION! MAYBE ONCE ALL OF YOU LITTLE SPARKS OF DIVINE LOVE HAVE FOUND YOUR WAY BACK HOME, I'LL LET Y'ALL HAVE A VOTE TO DECIDE! YOU CAN DECIDE IF LIFE IS WORTH THE COST! BETTER YET, JOBY, HOW ABOUT IF I LET YOU DECIDE? WHERE ARE YOUR WORDS, BELOVED? THE PROVERBIAL CAT GOT YOUR TOUNGE? SPEAK FOR YOUR BELOVED IS LISTENING!"

Joby's soul responded, "Like Job before me, I Job's daughter say as he said: 'I spoke without understanding of things beyond me, which I did not know. ... Therefore, I will recant and relent.'" "JOBY, MY BELOVED! OUR LOVE FOR EACH OTHER HAS BROUGHT US TOGETHER IN ONE BE-COM-ING. YOU ARE MY BELOVED! MY SPIRIT OF LOVE IS WITH YOU NOW AND FOREVERMORE!" After several minutes of awe-full silence passed, Joby opened her eyes as another gentle breeze caressed her as she rested in the proverbial peace that passes all understanding.

Later that night, Celeste came again and took Joby for another ride.

SWAN SONG FOUR

"My dear one Joby, how does it feel,
To hear our Beloved, could it be, was it real?
Your demand to be seen, to be near, to be heard,
Has been blessed by The Holy One, blessed by The Word.

Three questions you asked, 'Who, why, justify?'
All answered with Love, in God's sweet lullaby.
For Love to be real, for Love to be grown,
Spirit first must take form, only then is it known.

All of your questions went mute, your objections gone dumb,
You bowed there in silence, almost sucking your thumb.
Like Job before you, the suffering you've owned,
Was suddenly gone, with the wind it was blown.

You were then asked a question, 'Would you do it again?'
Would you write a new story, your life as the pen?
Is life worth the cost? What say – Yay or Nay?
Would you choose to come back – to see a new day?"

Then Joby said quietly, "Please, my dear friend.
No more questions or answers from me will you rend.
There's nothing to do, there's nothing to say.
I AM LOVE, I AM PEACE, I AM ONE WITH LOVE'S WAY."

Joby awoke with a smile in the darkest of night, grateful for the love she had experienced in these last few days.

DAY FORTY

On the last day of Joby's life, Theo returned as Joby had suggested. Not to his surprise he found Joshua, Monk, and even Eli in the room along with Jacob and Anna. Joby's breathing was shallow and intermittent and her eyes had been closed ever since her visitation by THE BELOVED. One by one, they moved to her side and shared their final words.

Eli was first and said, "Joby, forgive me for putting my values, my ideas, and my desires ahead of really listening to you. Our God of Love is full of mercy and grace. God knows your heart much better than I do. But I know it now to be good and true. Godspeed, my friend!"

Monk went next and smiled as he whispered, "Joby, my swan riding friend! Keep your eyes on the Light and allow no detours no matter how enticing they might be! Follow the Light to the Pure Land and know delight!"

Joshua simply stood by the top of Joby's bed and shared some loving energy with her by placing one hand above her forehead and holding the other above her heart.

Theo asked Anna and Jacob if they had any final words for Joby. Crying, Anna came to Joby's side and said, "My dear baby, flesh of my flesh. It's time for you to leave and soar with God's angels! I love you enough to say it's time for you to go!" Jacob went to the other side of Joby and wept, finally saying, "My wonderful wife, in joy and in strife, love of my life! Thank you! Thank you! Thank you!" The wounded bitterness in Joby's father's heart from the loss of his grandchildren and the soon to be loss of his daughter was preventing him from being with Joby. He had told her several weeks before, "Baby girl, forgive me, but I can't see you losing your life in front of my eyes. I need to remember you as you were." Joby had responded, "It's okay daddy, I know you love me, and know I love you."

Theo went to the foot of Joby's bed, took a deep breath and as he exhaled said, "Joby, receive The Spirit of Love." They were all amazed when Joby opened her eyes. But she did not look at any person in the room, not even Theo. Her eyes were joyously focused on The Light above Theo's head and the angels and her departed loved ones waiting therein. Taking three breaths, Joby quietly said loud enough for all to hear, "… I AM LOVE. … I AM PEACE. … I AM ONE WITH LOVE'S WAY." Joby then closed her eyes and said within as she exhaled her last breath, "BELOVED, receive my spirit."

For a few minutes no one moved, no one shared a word; they were still in the presence of her loving and peaceful soul.

POSTSCRIPT

Our play has now run, our tale has been told,
We've shared all our answers, for young and for old.
Our answers may not satisfy all, I'll confess.
But it's now time to ask, "Where is God in this mess?"

To know God is Love, so simple, so true!
With Love in God's heart, what else could God do?
God's question remains, would <u>you</u> do it again?
The suffering, the joy, the love, all the pain!

Have you tasted enough good of this life you can say?
"I'm thankful for life and all in this day!"
May The Spirit of Love guide you wherever you're at.
May you know and grow Love, like our beloved Jobat.

May it be so!

YESHUA'S LAMB

YESHUA'S LAMB

Miriam smiled as she saw her ten year old son running toward their home in the Galilean hills close to Mt. Carmel. "Mother, I saw the most wonderful thing today," Yeshua exclaimed. "I was walking in the fields and I saw a shepherd kneeling by a sheep. I ran over and it was a mother giving birth! Mother, I saw a baby lamb born today! It was yucky and beautiful at the same time. Even though the mom was tired and in pain the lamb's mother started licking the lamb. He was so bloody! After some time the lamb got up on its feet and started drinking his mother's milk. She was so tired and yet she stood there giving milk. It was awesome! I asked the shepherd if I could pet the lamb and he said it was okay. He was so soft and wet." Yeshua stopped talking and was silent for some time. He walked over to Miriam and looking into her eyes quietly asked, "When you gave birth to me and Yoachim and Rebecca did you have a lot of pain?" Miriam smiled and hugged Yeshua. Stepping back while still holding his shoulders she stated, "Yes son, there is pain in giving birth, but it left quickly because of the joy I felt in holding and nursing you. Life is a precious gift from

geoagape

The Holy One and we mothers are honored in our ability to give birth to Love. That is what you and all children and all baby lambs are – a gift of Love from The Holy One."

Yeshua did not immediately comment, but looked toward the field where the baby lamb was probably nursing. Mary asked, "What are you thinking about Yeshua?" He replied, "Mother, I know what's going to happen to that lamb. The shepherd is not like us. He believes that lambs are food and that special unblemished lambs are meant to be sacrificed at the Temple in Jerusalem. Like all outsiders they don't have reverence for life like we Nazoraeans do. Why can't they feel the wrong it is to take the lamb's life? How can they kill the lamb?" Yeshua started crying and tears began to fall from his eyes. "Why can't they know and see what we know and see? Why can't they have love in their hearts for the lambs like we do? Why do they have hearts of stone? We've never eaten meat! The lamb is so beautiful and so innocent. How could anyone kill it? What kind of heart does a person have who can kill a lamb?"

Miriam sighed and replied, "The shepherds and the outsiders live in a world with different values. Their scriptures say God ordered them to have lambs killed for Passover and have other animals killed for other sacrificial offerings at the Temple. We Nazoraeans believe their scriptures are false teachings and that God wants compassion and mercy for all beings in the creation. The outsiders kill because they have been taught for centuries by their culture that it's the right thing. Their hearts become closed to the suffering of the lamb. Most don't do the killing themselves. Most don't see the tortuous, bloody suffering of the animals being slaughtered. When they feast on the flesh of the lamb they try not to think of the lamb dancing, jumping and kicking in the field."

As Miriam wiped some tears from her son's eyes Yeshua asked, "Mother, how can a lamb be born to die?" Miriam caressed her son and holding him close to heart whispered into his ear, "Yes, my dear beloved son, indeed, how can a lamb be born to die?"

A few days later near sunset Yeshua came home and saw his father Yoseph in his carpenter's shop. "Father, I played today with the new lamb. We ran in the field together. I gave him a name. His name is Isa." Yoseph chuckled and said approvingly, "Isa for the prophet Isaiah. 'And the wolf shall lie down with the lamb. They shall not hurt nor destroy in all of my holy mountain for the earth shall be full of the knowledge of the Lord.' Yeshua, you know what's going to happen to Isa! He looks unblemished and is perfect for next year's Passover sacrifice. Maybe you shouldn't get too close to this lamb. Maybe giving him a name is not a good idea." "Father, I know we're Nazoraeans, but we're also Jews and as Jews we're supposed to go the Temple three times a year for the rituals. We go to Jerusalem and eat with our Essene brothers and sisters, but you've never taken me to the Temple yet. Why haven't you taken me to the Temple?" Yeshua asked.

Yoseph looked at his son, dropped his head, looked south to Jerusalem and sighed, "As Nazoraeans, it's a hard thing to witness. Yeshua, there's so much bleeting, bellowing, and moaning of the animals about to be sacrificed. They know what's happening all around them and they know they are next! They're terrified! There's so much blood being spurted from the animals' veins as the heart continues to pump. It becomes a river a blood! Yeshua, it's a river of ritual blood!" Yoseph wept. Yeshua walked over to his father and hugged him. Feeling the love in his son's embrace Yoseph sobbed with deep moans and groans feeling the pain, the terror, and the suffering of the sacrificed animals. After a few minutes, Yeshua sat his father on a chair, went outside for a cup of water and brought it to Yoseph. "Thank you, my son. Yeshua, my dear beloved son, you've been spared the sight of the Temple holocausts because it's a horrible sight for us who know that the other

geoagape

creatures of God's creation are neither meant to be our food nor our sacrifices. Once you hear their cries, once you see their deaths, once, you smell the blood, the urine, the feces, once you feel the terror in the air – you never forget it. It becomes part of you. It's horrible. Yeshua, I want to spare you and Yoachim that horror!" Yeshua responded, "Father, I am ten years old. In three years I will be a man. It's time I see more of the outside world. I need to experience what you have experienced. I need to experience the Temple Holocaust."

Yoseph responded, "My son, it's so overwhelming for us Nazoraeans! I get so emotional there when I see the suffering of the animals and birds. I cry and I get angry! My heart burns within me! At times I think about upsetting the cages of the birds and letting the animals go free. I feel like taking a whip to the people who are so uncaring. They are so thoughtless, so cruel! But then I remind myself – 'Yoseph, you are a husband and a father, you have a family for which you must care. Yoseph, if you lost control and acted like a righteous prophet you'd be arrested and probably stoned as a heretic.' Yeshua, what good would it do? The Temple priests have so many guards! The Romans kill troublemakers. We Nazoraeans are just few in numbers." Yeshua responded with resolve in his voice, "Father, I pray it will be God's will and yours for us to go to

the Temple Passover sacrifice next year. There's a voice within me saying I must experience it for myself. I believe it's the voice of the Shekinah father. I believe the Spirit is calling for me to make witness to this Holocaust myself."

A few months later, Yeshua and his younger brother Joachim were playing with Isa and the shepherd's other lambs in a field. After some joyous romping the boys laid down in the green pasture. Soon Isa came up to them and nuzzled Yeshua's elbow. Yeshua remarked, "Yoachim isn't it amazing! Psalm 23 has the image of God as a good shepherd. He takes care of us, protects us, leads us into green pastures, and provides us with all goodness. At the end it says, 'Mercy shall follow me all the days of my life.' How can the outsiders say that Psalm and then kill the lamb? That's not goodness, that's not mercy! They are unknowing, uncaring hypocrites!" Yoachim replied, "Yes brother, we are fortunate never to have eaten the flesh of another being of life killed for us. We've been taught, we know, that they are our neighbors and scripture says we should love our neighbor as ourself. Isa is one-half year old. Soon he'll be killed. Maybe we should take him from the shepherd. I know it's wrong to steal, but which is the greater sin – to steal or to kill? Wouldn't it be justified to save Isa's life?"

Yeshua pondered Yoachim's question and replied, "What good would it do? We are not going to kill Isa; the shepherd and the priests will do that and Isa's blood will be on their hands. If we stole Isa, the sin of stealing would weigh on our hearts. We might save Isa, but the shepherd would just take one of the other lambs and have it sacrificed. We'd get into trouble for breaking the Law. We might make trouble for other Nazoraeans. Father and mother have always taught us to have respect for the right of people to choose for themselves how to live – no matter how wrong they are and no matter how many bad decisions they make." Yeshua looked at the little lamb by his side and said, "Isa, we are born to die, some of us sooner than others. May our deaths have some meaning and purpose."

A half year later the time for Passover was near. Yoseph, Yeshua now eleven, and Yoachim joined the caravan of Galileans, including a large number of Nazoraeans and Essenes from the Mt. Carmel area on the three day journey to Jerusalem. Miriam did not join them for she was again with child. The shepherd who owned Isa was also in the group and allowed Yeshua and Yoachim to help him guide the Passover lambs south. Isa was now a one year old lamb and was unblemished. He had grown to be a wonderful lamb. He was one of about forty lambs being guided towards Jerusalem – to their deaths – to their holocausts!

Three days later they arrived. As always, when they came over the top of the hill and saw the gleaming gold of the Temple they stood in awe for a few seconds, watching the dazzling diamonds of reflected Temple light, watching the smoke curl up from the Temple altars, and being amazed at the swirl of human activity in and surrounding the Temple. At first Yoseph smiled, but then his countenance fell as he began to smell the smoke of the holocausts below. The shepherd quietly led Isa and the other sheep down the hillside and through the city gate. Soon they were on the Temple Mount and were guided into a holding area. The three Nazoraeans followed silently. Yeshua found Isa in the group of lambs and called to him. Isa heard Yeshua's voice and made his way to his friend. Yeshua reached through the wood fence and patted Isa on the nose, between the eyes, and between the ears on the top of his head. Yeshua said, "Isa, I'm sorry my friend for what will soon happen to you. I'm sorry we Nazoraeans haven't done enough to convince the outsiders that what they are doing is wrong. I hope your death will be swift. I call for the angels of mercy to have mercy on your soul and on the souls who will soon take your life. God doesn't want your blood. God wants mercy and compassion. God wants love. I love you Isa. I will remember you always."

After a few hours it was the shepherd's turn for Isa's sacrifice. Yeshua followed the shepherd as he led Isa to the Temple priests. Yeshua's senses were overwhelmed by what he saw, heard, and smelled around him. Scores of priests were in varying degrees of sacrificial holocaust. Some were tying the lambs' hind legs together, some were cutting the necks of the bleeting lambs, some were cutting the flesh into different portions – some for the sacrifice, some for the priests, and some for the evening's Passover meal. Blood was spurting from the necks of many upside down lambs and falling upon the priests who robes were drenched in blood. The lambs' blood was flowing under the hanging lambs. Yeshua was horrified. Suddenly, he saw a priest take Isa and tie his feet together and quickly swung his back legs over one of the horns of the altar. It seemed to Yeshua as if Isa was looking directly at him when with one deft slash of the ritual knife the priest cut Isa's throat and his heart started pumping his life-giving blood outspurt, by horrifying spurt. Yeshua left out a groan of grief and exclaimed, "Isa!" Yoseph came up from behind and placed his hands on Yeshua's shoulders. Instead of turning away into the comfort of his father's embrace, Yeshua forced himself to continue watching Isa's holocaust.

After Isa stopped kicking and the blood stopped draining, the priest took him off the hook, skinned him, and gave him to another priest in line who quietly carved him into pieces. As Yeshua watched, he heard the words of other Temple priests who were reciting Psalm 118:22 as Isa's sacrifice was completed: "The stone which the builders rejected has become the chief cornerstone. This is The LORD's doing; it is marvelous in our sight. This is the day that The LORD has made; let us exult and rejoice on it. O LORD, deliver us. O LORD, let us prosper. May he who enters be blessed in the name of The LORD; we bless you from the house of The LORD. The LORD is God; he has given us light; bind the festal offering to the horns of the altar with cords."

Yeshua walked over to the river of blood which flowed from the altar, bent down and put his hands in the blood of the lambs. Only one priest noticed in the midst of all of the activity, but he was aghast at Yeshua's "sinful" behavior. Yoseph quickly pulled Yeshua away and quickly walked away from the glaring priest. As they left the Temple area Yeshua shouted, "How can they do that? It's horrible! So many lambs! So much blood on their hands! So much death! God can't want that!" Yoseph quickly said, "Yeshua you must not say these things so loud and so close to the Temple. This is their way. We could get in trouble if any of the Temple guards hear you. There are just some things in life you have to live with – and die with."

Yoseph took Yeshua and Yoachim through the streets until they met at the gathering house of the Nazoraean Essenes. As they entered two men in white were startled when they saw Jesus and his hands and garments with blood on them. They quickly escorted them into a purifying area where they were washed and given white tunics. A few hours later, a Nazoraean elder convened their Passover Meal. They shared the bitter herbs which reminded them of their ancestors' time in Egyptian slavery. They shared the haroseth made of fruit and nuts which reminded them of the mortar which their ancestors were forced to make. They drank grape juice, for as Nazoraeans they drank no wine. In place of the Passover Lamb, they shared the unleavened bread.

Near the end of the meal, the Elder lifted a cup of grape juice, blessed it and said, "My brothers and sisters, may our Passover Meal remind us that all who breathe in the Spirit of God's breath are not free. May sacrificial death pass over all sentient beings allowing all to freely live their lives. May the Holocaust of the outsiders end. May Peace prevail. May we brothers and sisters live in peace." Yeshua joined his Nazoraean community in a whispered, "Amen."

One year later, Yeshua now twelve, once again joined the Passover caravan to the South. This time Miriam joined Yoseph, Yeshua, Yoachim, Rebecca, Yoses, and Yuda on the journey. After the three day journey, Yeshua immediately went into the Temple Mount and quietly watched the holocausts. With tears in his eyes and the blood of the holocaust smoke in his nostrils, he prayed a silent prayer, "Abba, I give thanks that I know this is not your will. Give me the wisdom to know how to show others this is not your will. Give me the strength to do your will so that this yearly Passover holocaust and the daily sacrificial holocausts of flesh end. Abba, may all beings know the happiness for which you created them. Amen"

Yeshua ate the Passover meal again with his fellow Nazoraeans that evening and several days later Yoseph led his family out of Jerusalem joining the caravan north to Galilee and the Nazoraean and Essene settlements surrounding Mt. Carmel. Yeshua started out with his family but, guided by the Spirit, he felt the urge to leave the caravan and go back to the Temple again. Instead of going to the Temple altar area Yeshua knew he should sit with the Rabbis and scholars and listen to them debate the meaning of the Law and the other scriptures. He listened intently and quietly for two days. On the morning of the third day he knew it was time for him to engage his elders. Yeshua knew he would be identified as a Nazoraean from Galilee by, his dialect, his white tunic, and the nature of his questions. He also knew he had to be careful not to offend any of his elder Jews with his comments. Guided by the Spirit, he began engaging the scholars of the traditional Law.

"My revered Rabbis and scholars of the Law. You have seen me here listening quietly and earnestly for two days now as you have so lovingly debated the meaning of The Holy One's scriptures. We who know and love our Father in Heaven, share many beliefs, but we also have considerable disagreements about many issues as has been evident over these past days. Our brother Sadducees recognize only the first five books of scripture. Our brother Pharisees argue that God's Spirit and Truth can be found in other writings, such as the Wisdom Writings and the Prophets. As you can see and hear, I am a Nazoraean and as such I was taught that some of the revered Law which many hold to be Holy is not truly the inspired word of God. As a child still one year away from becoming a son of the covenant, I seek you wisdom and your truth on this matter of knowing which scripture I should revere as from God and which I should see as the word of men put into the mouth of God. With so many differing opinions from so many God-fearing brothers from Abraham's loins, how am I, only a child, to know what is God's Word and what is not? For example, as you know, as a Nazoraean

I have been taught that animals were not meant by God to be our food and to be sacrificed."

Caiphas, a young priest, quickly interrupted Yeshua, "The sacrifices were clearly commanded by God through the great prophet Moses. In Leviticus he clearly gives us the sacred commandments concerning the sacrifices. Abraham was given a ram so that Isaac was saved from being sacrificed. There is no room for doubt in the Holy Scriptures. They are binding on all and any who cannot live by them are not Jews!" Another young man named Joseph of Arimathea who was from a wealthy family owning some merchant ships responded, "That's true my brother Caiaphas. Some scriptures clearly call for the sacrifice of animal flesh, but remember the original intention of God was for all of us, including animals, to eat the green of the fields. That's in the book of Genesis. He gave us seeds and nuts and the green of the fields for us all. The original plan was for there to be no killing and no taking of life. It was a Garden of Life not death." Caiaphas responded, "Yes, we all know that, but after the Great Flood, God allowed us to eat flesh." Yeshua listened to Caiaphas, Jospeh, and the many other elders who joined into the discussion for hours. When a pregnant silence settled over the men, moved by the Spirit, Yeshua asked, "As a Nazoraean I have been taught and I have lived by some scriptures on this issue which have guided me to this day. May I offer these prophetic voices to this dialogue in the hope that next year when I take upon myself the covenant I may truly know in my heart which words I will keep. Hear these prophetic voices: From Hosea [6:6] we hear, 'I desire steadfast love and not sacrifice, the knowledge of God, rather than burnt offerings.' From Amos [5:22] we hear, 'Even though you offer me your burnt offerings, I will not accept them.' My beloved Isaiah [1:11-13] says, 'I am sated with whole offerings of rams and the fat of buffaloes; I have no desire for the blood of bulls, of sheep and of goats. Whenever you come to enter my presence – who asked you for this? No more shall you trample my courts. The offer of your gifts is useless, the reek of sacrifice is abhorrent to me.' Finally, I ask you to consider what Jeremiah [7:22] says, 'But when I brought your forefathers out of Eqypt, I gave them no commands about whole-offering and sacrifice; I said not a word about them.'" How can all of these scriptures be the Word of God? Don't they contradict what is said in The Law? The prophets support the teachings of my fellow Nazoraeans. The Law, however, is equally clear. How am I, a child, to know what I must believe?" A troubled silence settled over the assembly. Pharisees, Sadducees, and Nazoraeans nervously looked at one another. Finally, and very cautiously, another young and respected member of the Sandhedrin named Nicodemus spoke saying, "Yeshua's words are sincere. I marvel how they come from one not yet a son of the covenant. My brothers, he means us no offense. We Jews have debated these questions for centuries and it appears our ancestors may be debating them after we become dust. Yeshua sincerely desires to know and do the will of God – just as we all desire. His heart is a heart which seems to be far more open to the suffering of the animals we see around us. Brothers, I must humbly admit that I too sometimes have trouble blocking out the cries of the animals as I try to settle down to sleep. Sometimes I say to myself, 'Woe to us who have eyes that see and ears that hear.' Then I hear a spiritual echo within, 'Woe to those have eyes and don't see and ears but do not hear.'" Again, a great silence covered the assembly.

Slowly from the back of the gathering a man and a woman approached Yeshua. It was Miriam and Yoseph. "Son, we have been worried about you. We thought you were with us in the caravan heading north. When after a day and one-half we discovered you were not with us we turned back to find you and discover you here debating the Law. Why have you treated us like this?" Miriam asked. Yeshua replied, "Did you not know I must be about Abba's work?" Yoseph looked painfully at Yeshua and Miriam lowered her head. Yeshua looked at their countenance and softly said, "I am still your child and I honor you and our way. But you must know I am preparing for the time to come when I am a man and I must leave your house. Let us go home to the green pastures of Galilee. It's time to play with the new born lambs getting big and fat for next year's holocaust." Saying this Yeshua rose, glanced at the Temple, smelled the smoke from the day's offerings, and followed his parents back to Galilee.

Upon the way, Yeshua remembered his lamb Isa drinking his mother's milk, jumping in the field, and nudging his elbow. He smiled as he remembered his friend, but his joy was soon turned to sorrow with the sudden memory of seeing his lamb hung upside down from the horns of the altar and having his throat slit by people who believed a blood sacrifice was necessary in order to be at peace with God. Yeshua knew in his heart that the prophets were right and blood sacrifice was invented by people and not willed by the God of Love who loved him and all beings equally.

As he walked, Yeshua said to himself, "May it be thy will, Abba, that somehow, some way, I will be an instrument to bring peace to people and to the animals and end their suffering." A little further up the road, a strong wind suddenly started blowing. He looked up and saw a dove circling above him. Yeshua smiled and said, "Hello, my beloved friend. Come Holy Spirit. Come Holy Breath." He took a deep breath and thought, "I AM the sun, I AM the dove, I AM the wind, I AM the lamb." He exhaled and breathing upon the world exclaimed, "O earth, earth, earth, hear the cries of the Lamb."

NEVER AGAIN

NEVER AGAIN

The following writing appeared as an
invited editorial on page 63 of the
Columbia Daily Tribune, Columbia,
MO., Sunday August 5, 1984.

"NEVER AGAIN": a plea for peace in the nuclear age.
A conscientious objector speaks his mind
By George Mummert
The writer, a doctoral candidate in philosophy
at the University of Missouri-Columbia
is a 1983 graduate of St. Paul School of Theology
in Kansas City. He is currently in the
Metropolitan Correctional Center in Chicago
for trespassing on Whiteman Air Force
Base during an anti-nuclear protest.

Hours before I was arrested, I talked with my two daughters about my decision not to cooperate with the conditions of my probation. I asked them if they understood what I did and why I did it. One answered, "Yeah, dad. You went across the line at Whiteman (Air Force Base in western Missouri) twice within the same year, and you were told not to. The judge put you on probation, but you've been talking with us the past few months about being uncomfortable with continuing to sign your month's report (probation papers). You said you might not be able to sign in the future and that your suspended sentence of five months and twenty-nine days would be taken away and you'd have to go to jail."

Then my other daughter said, "You know dad, it's like <u>Horton Hears A Who.</u> Do you know that book by Dr. Seuss? It's a story about an elephant who sees a flower that contains a world of little people who call themselves Whos, and the name of their home is Whoville. The Whos see that Horton is going to pick up and blow on their beautiful flower so they realize they need to shout as loud as they can so that Horton can hear them and not destroy them. Then they found one little Who who was practicing his music lessons and who hadn't shouted. They got him to join them in shouting that they wanted to live. Horton heard them and stopped. That's what you and your friends are trying to do. You're trying to get everyone in the whole wide world to shout at the same time that we want to live so that we don't die in a nuclear war."

I fought back the tears, swallowed the lump in my throat, and we eventually shared hugs and kisses secure in the knowledge that the memories of our past and the promise of our future would be sufficient to sustain our love for each other in the present half- year in which we are physically separated.

During the first few weeks in jail, I received many letters that posed the same basic question. "Why did you do civil disobedience and not work within the system?" "Why couldn't you sign your probation papers and do the community service?" "Why now?"

For those who do not appreciate Dr. Seuss, I shall attempt a response.

Very simply, there came a point in my life when I knew that I could no longer be "an aimless well-behaved spectator." I knew I had voted, had written letters, had signed petitions, had prayed for peace and I had even served the country in alternative service as a conscientious objector during the Vietnam War, but I realized that these actions were no longer sufficient to express my love for life, my growing pain and sorrow concerning the plight of the poor and our inadequate response to that plight, and my growing fear of a probable nuclear holocaust. I kept seeing the nuclear spring being wound tighter and tighter and felt as if the hot nuclear summer, our nuclear fall, and the nuclear winter that scientists discussed could not be far away.

As my very best friend called it when it when she first felt it passing by a missile silo, I had experienced "The Big No." When she said that, I added, "The Big Know." We had seen too many hungry and homeless people, too many religious people praying for peace and paying for war, and too many missile silos. After my "Big Know" in October of 1981, I knew I could no longer be "well behaved" concerning some of my government's policies.

For example, I knew I could no longer pay all my federal income taxes because some of it would be used to buy weapons of death and to train people to use them and to kill in my name even though I refused to use them myself. I realized that even though the government did not draft my body for Vietnam, it had drafted my tax dollars. I also knew that some more of my tax dollars were buried beneath the green fields of western Missouri – poised for flight and no more than thirty minutes away from millions of innocent men, women, children and other life forms in the Soviet Union.

Consequently, it was important for me to begin a walk August 6th, 1982 in Kansas City at the Federal Internal Revenue Service Collection Center next to the Bendix Corporation (a nuclear bomb component manufacturer) complex and to conclude my walk three days later at Whiteman, which controls one hundred and fifty Minutemen missiles. I walked in remembrance of all war dead, but especially remembered the dead of Hiroshima and Nagasaki. I heard from deep within me the solemn words that are written on the Hiroshima memorial stone – "Never Again." On the evening of August 9th I knew I had to cross the artificial boundary in civil disobedience. Again on April 22, 1983 I knew I had to celebrate Earth Day at Whiteman. With a community of faith I celebrated a meal of Shalom – a meal of wholeness – in thanksgiving for our beautiful home and for the wondrous gift of life. When the meal was over, I went to the boundary with another companion. We knelt and prayed. I then bent over and kissed the Earth where I would plant a flower of peace. As rain gently blessed our witness, we crossed the boundary in the spirit of boundless love.

Even though those two steps have resulted in my being "secured" by the federal government in a "Correctional Center" for one-half year, those steps were "steps of freedom" on the way of love. For those two steps I was given a suspended sentence of five months and twenty-nine days, two years of probation and one hundred hours of community service. I never signed the Conditions of Probation Statement which stated, "I will abide by the above conditions." I believe that if we do not do something soon about nuclear weapons, there will no longer be any community to serve. I look upon my half-year in prison as a form of community service. One might say it is a "tour of duty" or better yet, a "service of love" on behalf of the beloved community.

I knew then that I would probably have to take another "step of freedom" because the philosophy of civil disobedience suggests that the proponent be prepared to serve the maximum possible sentence. For example, Gandhi told his judges to give him the harshest sentence if they believed in their laws of colonialization. Consequently, I knew that I could not do community service that the government "approved." I was already serving the community in various ways.

Ultimately, I realized I could no longer cooperate with a system that is legalizing the nuclear destruction of the Earth. The legal system protects the weapons of nuclear death with its "No Trespassing" laws and the many barbed-wire fences that attempt to keep the U.S. people away – almost like the German people were kept outside the concentration camps of a past holocaust. But we will not have the excuse, "We did not know what they were doing." The nuclear superpowers are both guilty of nuclear terrorism; the people of the Earth have been held hostage for almost thirty-nine years.

The word "probation" means to test. The government was literally testing my faithfulness, and for the months that I cooperated, I felt I was not passing the test. From August 1983 through March 1984, I signed eight monthly probation reports. Each time I signed, I felt more guilt, but I rationalized it by saying I had commitments to this or that and that I had a responsibility to my family. In those eight months, I saw more missiles moved into Europe and subs perched closer to the U.S. coast. I also know that twenty-four million people starved to death.

Finally, on the day that I signed and mailed my last probation report, I heard the news that our government would be conducting another underground nuclear test in Nevada. At the appointed hour, I walked outside. I could not literally feel the Earth shake, but as I stood there, I heard from deep within, "Never Again." Thus when I failed to sign my report for March, I was arrested. Through the paradox of suffering love, I am empowered to express at the same time the death-denying "Big No" and the life- affirming "Big Yes."

In the year between the 39th and 40th anniversaries of the atomic bombing, we will once again have many chances to choose between life and death. In August, all over the world, millions will remember and say, "Never Again." Some people will again

geoagape

make the walk from Kansas City to Whiteman in order to witness with their bodies to their hope in a world free of war and hunger. They will also walk in memory of the 200,000 people who immediately lost their lives in Hiroshima and Nagasaki. One of the Hiroshima survivors has written, "That number of dead is hard to imagine. Conceive, however, of placing them side by side, giving twenty inches per body, and they would stretch sixty miles." The walk from Kansas City, the scene of "The Day After," is sixty miles. With every step they take, the walkers will be remembering one more nuclear victim.

For some their steps will be completed with another "step of freedom" into the world of boundless love and out of a world where boundaries separate one from another. In the year ahead, we can choose to love the poor or to continue our selfish lifestyles. In November, we can choose new direction for our government or continue the present one. In April we can choose to say to the IRS "Never Again" or we can continue to pay for war.

Many will say, "What about the Soviets?" It is my belief that the United States has a moral responsibility to take the leadership in the attempt to defuse the arms race because we were the first country to use atomic weapons. Our country must demonstrate moral vision and imagination if the cycle of violence is to cease. We need more pairing projects and large group visits to each other's homelands. We need face- to-face meetings, which are both imaginative and experiential between our governments' leaders. For example, I think it's a good beginning to be meeting in Geneva to discuss peace for space, but I wonder what would happen if our representatives met in space to discuss peace.

As another example, I make this proposal. It's based on the fact that for people worldwide, bread is a symbol of life. It is also based on the Soviet custom of presenting guests with a loaf of bread and some salt. I propose an experiential meeting called "The Bread and Salt Talks." [For younger readers, SALT (Strategic Arms Limitation Treaty) Talks were being held in the 1980s.]

During the upcoming fall, I urge the leaders of both governments, or groups from each country if the leaders refuse, to exchange visits and plant some of their native winter wheat in each other's country. Preferably, both leaders would assist each other in preparing the soil, and both would assist each other in the planting of the seeds. Then in the spring or early summer, if my agrarian advisor is correct, the leaders could meet again in each other's countries to share in the harvest of the wheat. They could then proceed to the Northern Pacific's Bering Strait, where the Soviet island of Ostrov Ramanova and the U.S. island of Little Diomede appear to be no more than five or ten miles apart.

The leaders of each country could then do on each other's coast what Gandhi did a half century ago – make salt from the common sea. Having made the salt, they could proceed to the kitchen of a United Nations ship, which would be positioned between the two islands. Then the leaders could blend the wheat from the two countries and bake loaves of bread that could symbolize our common humanity and love of life. A joyous celebration could then be consummated by toasting the success of the Bread & Salt Talks with Soviet vodka and wine from the United States. Imagine what could be said while plowing, planting, harvesting, milling, and baking the bread! Picture the leaders raising the salt from the sea as Gandhi did! Imagine the new beginning when the bread, salt, vodka and wine are shared with each other!

Many will say, "Impossible" or "That's the most foolish idea I've ever hear." But I say, "Bread and Salt can talk." If the leaders refuse to participate in the Bread & Salt Talks, then I say now what someone has said before, "When the people are willing to lead, eventually the leaders will follow." I even know a farmer in Missouri who would allow some Soviet winter wheat to be planted in his field which holds one of the Minuteman missiles.

In conclusion, with some measure of poetic license and with thanks to the spirit of Ezekiel (and Dr. Seuss), I offer this vision of decision:

Now it came to pass in the 38th year in the 10th month, as I was among the captives by the river of Chicago, that the cosmos was opened up, and I saw a vision of decision. The way of Love took me up from the Earth, and I heard, "Child of Earth, what do you see?" And I saw a beautiful wholeness of blue, brown, green and white. Then I heard, "Child of Earth, ye shall now see the choice of death or life for which you and your sisters and brothers are responsible. Thou shalt say unto them, 'Thy time of decision is close at hand.'"

Then, behold, I heard a thundering noise, and I saw a city burning, and lo I saw a fiery cloud consume the Earth. My tears could not quench the flames. With a broken heart, I heard, "Child of Earth, this is one vision of what can be. Now behold, see and hear another."

And lo, I beheld the Earth again in its wholeness and beauty. And I saw two crafts rise from opposite sides of the Earth, and they approached each other. And the two became one. And I heard the leaders of the two peoples wonder at the beauty of their home below. They joyously agreed they could not see any boundaries between the islands on the one sea. They knew the Wholeness of the Earth and felt as one in their hearts. They knew they were children of the one Earth – the home of care we all share. Then they formed a new covenant of peace. And I saw them seal their covenant with bread, salt, vodka, and wine. And I heard them say solemnly to one another, "Never Again." And then I heard them joyously shout with all the Children of Earth that they wanted to live. And my tears of joy fell upon the Earth, and a bow of colors appeared. And behold, I saw a new cosmos and a new Earth.

POSTSCRIPT

The Show Me Peace Walk continued for another ten years. It was nourished by many individual peacemakers and by two organizations – The Kansas City Interfaith Peace Alliance and The Hearthaven Community. Every year twenty to fifty walkers gathered to tread or support the sixty mile peace walk, to remember the victims of Hiroshima and Nagasaki, to nurture each other's souls, and to gather at the gate of Whiteman Air Force Base saying, "Never Again."

I'm happy to say that in 1995 the government removed the one hundred and fifty Minutemen II missiles and the fifteen hundred nuclear warheads from the base. I like to think that our constant twenty five year witness and prayers for peace were answered. Unfortunately, WAFB became a home for the B-2 bomber. The Show Me Peace Walk ended with the removal of the missiles, because they were the original reason for the witness.

Only the Spirit knows if a reunion walk is in the future.

In 1989, after much soul searching, I settled with the IRS and paid my back "war taxes" along with added penalty and interest. Hopefully, the government will soon recognize the right

geoagape

of conscientious objectors to not have their taxes be used in ways which contradict their religious beliefs. This may be done by passing The World Peace Tax Fund Bill which has been placed before Congress for more than three decades now. May it be so.

RECOMMENDED BOOKS

Katye Anna: Birthing Into Spirit.
Conscious Construction of the Soul.
Soul Love Never Ends.
Crossroads: Living a Soul Inspired Life.

Keith Akers: The Lost Religion of Jesus: Simple Living and Nonviolence in Early Christianity.

Will Tuttle: The World Peace Diet.

Coming in Summer of 2017 from geoagape:

What Would Jesus Eat Today? The Spiritual Vegan Way.
Awaking With Compassion: Daily Meditations for Spiritual Vegans and Those on the Way.

ABOUT THE AUTHOR

geoagape (pronounced "ja-ga-pay") is the spiritual name of the author who is more commonly known as George Mummert. He is a graduate of Catawba College (BA), The University of Toledo-Ohio (MA), Saint Paul School of Theology (M.Div.), and The University of Missouri-Columbia (Ph.D.).

He is the proud father of two wonderful daughters, Caryn and Melissa, and the proud grandfather of Jack, Laura, and Annie. Maggie, his faithful and loving four-legged friend rescued him.

While serving several small churches and participating in actions for peace and justice, he primarily taught philosophy and religion courses - four years as a teaching assistant at Mizzou and twenty-eight years at Moberly Area Community College. In 1984 he served a sentence of six months at the federal Metropolitan Correction Center in Chicago for federal trespassing at Missouri's Whiteman Air Force Base because of two civil disobedience witnesses against nuclear weapons.

After forty years of "wandering in the wilderness" of Missouri, he retired to "the promised land" of Myrtle Beach, SC for two wonderful, warm winter, writing years amid his wondrous, waving palms.

He became an ovo-lacto vegetarian in 1981 and in 2016 after reading Will Tuttle's <u>The World Peace Diet</u> became a vegan. He now identifies himself as a "vegan peacemaker," a "spiritual vegan," and a "vegan voice."

After surviving being flooded during South Carolina's "one-thousand year" flood in 2015 and surviving 2016 Hurricane Matthew's eyewall passing directly over his home, he has now been inspired to seek or develop a community for spiritual vegans in the state of New York, hopefully, near The Farm Animal Sanctuary and Ithaca.